PRAISE FOR *THE SPIRIT OF FATHERHOOD*

"I became a dad twenty years ago, but I became a father after I was introduced to Larry and his incredible principles. There is no greater undertaking you'll have as a man than being a father. Grabbing this book will all but guarantee you get it right."

—**Anthony Trucks, former NFL player and founder of Dark Work**

"This book should be considered essential reading for every man embarking on his fatherhood journey. Larry Hagner offers a wealth of experiences distilled into practical, real-life applications. He adeptly draws from his own experiences as well as insights gleaned from thousands of other fathers he has interviewed over the years."

—**Jake Herbert, 2009 world silver medalist, 2012 Olympian, two-time university world bronze medalist, 2009 Big Ten Athlete of the Year, and 2009 Dan Hodge Trophy recipient**

THE SPIRIT OF FATHERHOOD

Larry Hagner

Morehouse Publishing, 19 East 34th Street, New York, NY 10016

Morehouse Publishing is an imprint of Church Publishing Incorporated.

Cover design by Albert Tang
Typeset by Nord Compo

Library of Congress Cataloging-in-Publication Data

Names: Hagner, Larry, author.
Title: The spirit of fatherhood / Larry Hagner.
Description: New York, NY : Morehouse Publishing, [2024] | Includes
    bibliographical references.
Identifiers: LCCN 2024001909 | ISBN 9781640657113 (pbk) | ISBN
    9781640657120 (ebook)
Subjects: LCSH: Fatherhood—Religious aspects—Christianity. |
    Parenting—Religious aspects—Christianity.
Classification: LCC BV4529.17 .H34 2024 | DDC 248.8/421—dc23/
    eng/20240216
LC record available at https://lccn.loc.gov/2024001909

To my wife, Jessica:
Thank you for your unwavering example of faith and family. This book and mission wouldn't be possible without you.

To my four boys, Ethan, Mason, Lawson, and Colton:
You are my purpose for being on this earth. Being a part of your lives has been the best adventure anyone could ask for. I love you!

CONTENTS

INTRODUCTION

Welcome, fathers, to the magnificent, messy, heart-aching, incredible journey of fatherhood. Welcome home.

If possible, I urge you to open this book not with a mind seeking solutions but with a heart longing for connection. Within the following pages, you will find not answers but echoes, resonances of your own journey and those who came before you. For in the tapestry of fatherhood, we are not alone. We are woven together, stitch by stitch, by the invisible, unbreakable thread of love and shared experience.

From what I've been able to glean over the years of observing, speaking to, and listening to dads is that love is the lighthouse in the child's storm, the steady beacon of their heart against the chaos of the world. You are the sun that warms their spirit, the earth that nourishes their roots. You are, quite simply, everything.

As you have learned (or are about to learn), the dynamic between a father and child is like a fragile rhythm. It's a dance between awe and trepidation, a melody composed of hope and backed by a drumbeat of vulnerability. In its nascent dawn, fatherhood can feel like a universe contained in a single gaze. I wanted to write a testament to that singular gaze and give my fellow dads a kind of unfurled map that could roughly guide them through the tangled wilderness of being a parent. Each chapter can be considered a compass needle, drawn magnetically toward the north star of a child's love. Here, we'll delve not into mere tactics but into the profound art and alchemy of fatherhood, where clumsy hands cradle dreams and whispered stories shape souls. This map will not help you avoid all the pitfalls and quagmires of raising a kid. And if such a tool existed, I wouldn't recommend it, anyway! The stumbles and scars are a necessary part of the journey, and so are the canyons of doubt that you'll find yourself in after the falls. But within those shadows, too, lies the fertile soil of transformation. For a father's journey is not one of conquest but of surrender, a patient yielding to the unfurling mystery of another human being.

On this expedition, the best anyone can do is walk alongside you and I hope this book can be your companion, whether you're roaming the sunlit plains of laughter, braving the storm-tossed nights of worry, or tiptoeing through the quiet corridors of disappointment. For in these everyday moments, a father's love builds cathedrals of resilience within a child's heart.

To be clear, this is not a manual or a rulebook. It is an offering, a testament to the raw and exquisite vulnerability that defines fatherhood. It is a quiet chorus of voices, each sharing the poignant orchestration of guiding a soul, of watching a small hand reach for the vast expanse of the universe, knowing somehow it is your own hand they seek.

Having talked to and coached thousands of dads, I'm also keenly aware that in the depths of every father's heart lies a profound and transformative superpower, one that can shape lives, mold character, and leave an indelible mark on the world. It is a power that can seemingly defy the laws of physics and spark—from absolute nothingness— joy, vulnerability, growth, pain, happiness, trauma, and love. The cliché in this case is, indeed, true: with tremendous power, comes more responsibility than we can fathom. Often, the power we wield can be alienating, leading to moments of chilling solitude. Nights, swallowed by darkness, where questions gnaw at the edges of your soul: "Am I enough? Am I doing this right?" And it's in these existential valleys, where the words of this book will call out to you, like the strangely comforting echo of thunder in the distance.

As you'll see, each chapter delves into a certain aspect of fatherhood. We explore the art of developing compassionate communication, understanding the power of words, and creating intellectual connections with our children. We discover the importance of nurturing aspirations and guiding our children toward purposeful paths in life. We learn the significance of forgiveness, embracing imperfections, and finding true fulfillment beyond material possessions.

Throughout, you will find personal stories and reflective questions. As you may have already noticed, you'll also find an abundance of metaphors. This is necessary because the language of fatherhood—if one exists—is not one of cold equations and clinical pronouncements. It's a concerto of whispers, echoing between dawn laughter and bedtime stories. It's a canvas of strokes, alive and occasionally chaotic, crafting pictures of scraped knees and boundless dreams. When we discuss this sacred bond, facts feel as clumsy as a toddler in tap shoes. We turn to metaphor not as a crutch but as a soaring wing, because fatherhood is more an art than a science. As much as we might wish it were otherwise, in the crucible of childrearing, there are no predetermined formulas, no guaranteed outcomes. We navigate uncharted waters, guided by love's flickering flame and the echo of intuition. To share our experience, metaphors are our only compass—which is why I mentioned it above. After all, a father's heart is a kaleidoscope. To capture its multifaceted beauty, plain words fall short. Accordingly, to fully capture the experience, I might borrow from the rustling of the wind through trees, the crashing of waves on the beach, the silent constellations dancing in the vast expanse of night. These images hold the echoes of our own emotions, allowing us to connect, heart to heart, with the fathers who walk this path beside us.

So let us celebrate the language of fatherhood, not as a mere adornment but as a bridge across the chasms of experience. Within its verses, we discover

not solutions but a collective melody. Never forget that fatherhood is not a problem to be solved.
Instead, accept it as a mystery to be embraced, or, to
use another metaphor, a canvas to be drawn upon.

Sincerely, I hope that, over the years, these
pages will become a sanctuary for readers, a space
to pause, reflect, and draw inspiration. They might
even serve as a reminder that the impact of a father's
spirit extends far beyond his immediate family.

This campfire companion, crackling with the
wisdom of fathers past and present, can gently
remind us that the struggles and triumphs of fatherhood are a universal language, a secret handshake
across generations. So turn the page. Surrender to
the narratives as they roll in, like moonlit waves
along a serene shore. Welcome the challenges boldly,
for they will refine and fortify your spirit. And as
you embark on this extraordinary journey, remember: you are not alone. We stand side by side, fathers
united in the boundless love that burns within us.

Welcome to the brotherhood. Now let the spirit
of fatherhood guide you home.

CHAPTER 1

THE DAWN OF FATHERHOOD

A sense of anticipation hangs heavy in the air, a mix of excitement and trepidation. It's the feeling that washes over you when you stand on the precipice of a new adventure. This is the dawn of fatherhood. It's time to shed the pretense of having all the answers, to embrace the exhilarating unknown and the thrill of learning on the fly. Cast aside the anxieties of "what-ifs" and "how-tos," for fatherhood is a new chapter in a book yet to be written, a voyage into uncharted territory.

Think of it like this: you're a pioneering captain, charting a course through unmapped waters. You'll discover hidden strengths, develop skills you never knew you possessed, and learn to navigate the currents of life with newfound determination. You'll prioritize, plan, and provide in ways you never imagined possible, harmonizing your roles as a father, partner, and individual. But don't be fooled into thinking this journey is all smooth sailing. Parenthood demands a shift in priorities. The spontaneous outings, the carefree days of yore, may become less frequent. In their place, however, bloom moments of unparalleled beauty and tenderness: the first gurgle of laughter, the innocent touch of a tiny hand, the boundless wonder in a child's eyes.

These are the moments that redefine freedom, that paint life with vibrant colors. They teach us the depths of our own love, the fierce protectiveness that lies dormant within. For those of us who carry the scars of challenging childhood experiences, fatherhood offers a unique opportunity to rewrite our own story, to build the kind of relationship we always dreamed of. Here, amidst the chaos and the laughter, we discover the profound power of vulnerability. We learn to shed our armor, to show our emotions without reservation, and in doing so, we forge deeper connections with those we love.

Fatherhood is, after all, so many things. It's a new dawn of responsibilities, pains, and joys, which is why the role instantly encompasses so much of our being and identity. Along with it comes great responsibility and power, as well as a tremendous amount of fear. Accordingly, a new father must quickly evolve, and grow. A new dad needs to embrace change, as the path forward is going to be one of discovery, where apprehensions are a kind of stepping stone to a place of deeper understanding about yourself and your world. The experience is as beautiful as it is complex, and as scary as it is holy. But, also, entirely worth it.

Over the years, I've worked with thousands of dads and have noticed many common themes when they learn a child is on the way. They worry that they won't be good enough or know how to fulfill their responsibilities. They may fear not having all the answers or making mistakes that could negatively impact their children. In this new and uncharted territory, they worry about how their lives will change, how they'll adapt to new routines, and what challenges they'll face. Providing is a significant concern for any parent. The financial responsibilities of raising children, including education, healthcare, and general expenses, can create stress and worry.

Many stress about being able to balance their roles as fathers, husbands, and professionals. The pressure to excel in all areas of life can often be overwhelming, especially since parenthood comes with a certain kind of loss of personal freedom and independence. With a child in tow, new parents will fret about not being able to pursue their hobbies, interests, or social activities as freely as before.

Of course, concerns about the health and safety of the child never go away. I don't have to remind anyone of the dangers that lurk all around our corners—which can sometimes even include us, the father. Some of us grew up in difficult homes and we will struggle to not repeat the same negative patterns or mistakes. Fatherhood often requires emotional openness and vulnerability, and many men might not be used to expressing their feelings, fearing that it could make them appear weak or undermine their authority.

Some fear that the dynamic of their relationships will change after having children, potentially leading to less time and attention for each other. This is particularly true during the early stages of infancy, when many think they might not be able to connect with their own child, no less their partner.

Relationships will evolve, that's inevitable. The arrival of a child reshapes the entire landscape of our lives. But fear not, for these changes aren't always for the worse. Often, our partnerships grow stronger, forged in the crucible of shared responsibility and unconditional love. So, remember, the dawn of fatherhood isn't just about the challenges; it's about embracing them, growing through them, and discovering the profound joy and love that come with being a dad.

CONFIDENCE EMERGES: *PREPARING FOR FATHERHOOD*

The sterile air of the hospital room hummed with anticipation. A palpable tension filled the space, a mixture of excitement and terror swirling around you. This was it: the precipice of fatherhood.

The meticulously crafted plans, the mountains of parenting books devoured, the whispered advice from seasoned dads—they all evaporated in the face of your newborn's first cry. A raw, primal sound that ripped through the carefully constructed facade of your preparedness, leaving you feeling naked and exposed. Fear, that insidious serpent, began its ascent, slithering up your spine and coiling around your heart. Each gurgle, each whimper, each demand is like a relentless indictment of your inadequacy. Fatherhood, you realized with a jolt, was far less about sterile instructions and perfectly executed plans, and far more about a chaotic, improvisational dance with uncertainty.

It's a tango with exhaustion, a waltz with self-doubt, and a foxtrot with the ever-present fear of failure. You stumble, you fall, you question your every decision, and feel like you've regressed to a sleep-deprived, drool-covered pre-fatherhood version of yourself. But with each step backward, you discover something remarkable. A hidden strength, an unimaginable capacity for love, a wellspring of selflessness you didn't know existed. Fatherhood is a crucible, a furnace that burns away your imperfections and exposes your raw vulnerability. It forces you to confront your deepest fears and emerge stronger, wiser, and more resilient.

The endless to-do lists, the babyproofing projects, the late-night feedings—they become mere surface noise. Beneath it all lies a deeper, more spiritual journey, a quest for meaning and purpose driven by the cries and laughter of your child. Experience, hope, and a deep-seated faith become your guiding lights, the pillars upon which you build your confidence and navigate the uncharted waters of fatherhood. You learn to trust your instincts, to find your own unique rhythm in the chaos, and to embrace the unpredictable nature of life.

Fatherhood is not a meticulously choreographed performance; it's a messy, unpredictable, exhilarating adventure. It's a testament to the human spirit's capacity to adapt, to find joy in the simple moments, and to discover the extraordinary within the ordinary. Accordingly, the fear of inadequacy you will encounter at the beginning often comes from a natural yet deep-rooted anxiety. The thought, however, of not being enough for our children can be devastating, as many of us who have children consider the role of parent to be our most important. Feeling inadequate in that department can seem like the ultimate failure.

In these moments, I often found myself turning to the Bible—the following passages, in particular:

Isaiah 41:10: "So do not fear, for I am with you; do not be dismayed, for I am your God. I will strengthen you and help you; I will uphold you with my righteous right hand."

Psalm 46:1: "God is our refuge and strength, an ever-present help in trouble."

Matthew 11:28–30: "Come to me, all you who are weary and burdened, and I will give you rest. Take my yoke upon you and learn from me, for I am gentle and humble in heart, and you will find rest for your souls. For my yoke is easy and my burden is light."

Our sense of inadequacy tends to be amplified by solitude. God's message, however, is clear and constantly reminds us that we aren't alone and never will be alone. This can be hard to accept for a new father, as society has wired us to believe that men are supposed to be self-sufficient. Becoming a dad can make you feel all kinds of ways. But after a while, and with God's help, you start feeling surer of yourself. Again, the confidence doesn't show up overnight. It takes time and comes from the experiences you go through, problems you work out, and knowing you've got support.

Just as with our children, we too learn as they grow. We become less fearful and doubtful. We feel more assured. When you're a dad, confidence isn't about having all the answers and being perfect. Not even close. It is simply about having the peace of mind to be present, involved and willing to learn—always guided by faith, love, and the knowledge that you will learn from your mistakes.

HOPE IS ON THE HORIZON: *EMBRACING THE UNKNOWN*

As fathers, we can often feel hardwired to want certainty in everything: our health, finances, careers, and relationships. Deep down inside, we all want to be in control. We want to know what comes next, so that we can anticipate it. Accordingly, fear of the unknown is something everyone has experienced.

We don't necessarily enjoy surprises, unless, of course, they are pleasant. In fact, the surprises we don't enjoy are called "problems." But here's a simple idea: what if embracing surprises and the unknown laid out before all of us is where the real adventure of fatherhood begins? Find that silver lining in not knowing. Own that kind of mindset and you'll start to notice that the most unexpected moments bring the greatest joy.

The scriptures offer comforting words about facing the unknown:

Psalm 23:4: "Even though I walk through the darkest valley, I will fear no evil, for you are with me; your rod and your staff, they comfort me."

Matthew 6:34: "Therefore do not worry about tomorrow, for tomorrow will worry about itself. Each day has enough trouble of its own."

Joshua 1:9: "Have I not commanded you? Be strong and courageous. Do not be afraid; do not be discouraged, for the LORD your God will be with you wherever you go."

The unknown scares all of us to some degree, and there is no promise of a problem- and pain-free life. There will be suffering. There will be loss. We don't know what tomorrow has in store for us. The road ahead is unknown and some of the best-laid plans can and will go off the rails. Hope, however, is always on the horizon because we do not have to walk this journey alone. We can take heed that God has a plan and will not abandon us. Every step into the unknown is a chance to become stronger, more durable, and even more deeply connected with our offspring. But the mystery is more than a challenge; it's a blank slate for forging those lovely and unexpected moments that make our lives as dads so rich.

Let's try and approach every new day with a certain kind of boldness. We will stay hopeful that every new dawn will bring us more chances to get better. Hope is always out there on the horizon. Along with the divine, it will escort us through the darkness and into the light.

FISCAL HARMONY: *TRANSFORMING ANXIETY INTO FINANCIAL RESPONSIBILITY*

In some way, shape, or form, financial stress will always be a significant dynamic in our lives. The desire for financial security and the want to provide for our families is deeply ingrained in us as fathers. When we feel we're not meeting certain societal expectations, we tend to become deeply disappointed in ourselves, a pain that can shake us to our very core. Concern is understandable, too, especially in a world where costs always rise while wages and income seem to stay the same.

Financial distress and poor money management can contribute to major issues in any household. To make sure we don't become victims, we need to turn worry into wisdom, uncertainty into understanding, and financial challenges into responsible management. We need to align our financial practices with our values. A harmonious and sustainable path forward, for both ourselves and our families, is one that aligns with what we want in life and who we are as people, family members, and, of course, fathers.

What God says about financial stress:

Matthew 6:25–27: "Therefore I tell you, do not worry about your life, what you will eat or drink; or about your body, what you will wear. Isn't life more than food, and the body more than clothes? Look at the birds of the air; they do not sow or reap or store away in barns, and yet your heavenly Father feeds them. Are you not much more valuable than they? Can any one of you by worrying add a single hour to your life?"

Matthew 6:33–34: "But seek first his kingdom and his righteousness, and all these things will be given to you as well. Therefore do not worry about tomorrow, for tomorrow will worry about itself. Each day has enough trouble of its own."

Philippians 4:19: "And my God will meet all your needs according to the riches of his glory in Christ Jesus."

The stress that comes along with financial uncertainty is nothing short of dangerous. It can devastate us mentally, emotionally, physically, and even spiritually. However, we must always remember that God has blessed us with unique talents and abilities, enabling us to not only bring value to the lives of others, but also find creative ways to provide. These gifts are a testament to God's provision, even when a situation can seem dire from an earthly standpoint. Even when it comes to money, God reassures us that we do not have to take this journey alone.

By leaning on our faith and recognizing our God-given strengths, we can navigate the financial wilderness with a sense of harmony.

THE SYMPHONY OF LIFE: *BALANCING PARENTHOOD AND PERSONAL TIME*

In the symphony of life, parental responsibilities and personal freedoms rarely exist in perfect harmony. As we know, along with raising a child comes a monumental amount of extra work. Before kids, life likely seemed simpler. We had more freedom to do what we wanted when we wanted. The demands of other responsibilities just never felt as urgent. The simplicity of the pre-children life, with its abundant freedoms and lack of demands, can quickly become a distant memory. To make matters even more complicated, many of us never identify certain roles and responsibilities in the family. For whatever reason, we don't plan and simply expect things will get done. We fall into the trap of unspoken expectations, assuming it'll just be obvious who will do what. As a result, misunderstandings can cause resentment within the family.

What God says about balancing the workload:

Galatians 6:2: "Carry each other's burdens, and in this way you will fulfill the law of Christ."

1 Corinthians 11:11–12: "In the Lord, however, woman is not independent of man, nor is man independent of woman. For as woman came from man, so also man is born of woman. But everything comes from God."

We live in a busy world. Between work, family, and our personal goals, there are tremendous demand on our time. The to-do lists are never ending, echoing like a relentless drumbeat in the background of our daily lives. Something always needs to be fixed and it can seem like whenever you finally get around to the repair, something else breaks.

You will need help. Taking care of, and raising, a child properly requires a village, no matter how "strong" the father is. The best kind of help is the kind that is figured out in advance, has a strategy, and is communicated clearly. There is one thing that, like a cancer, can metastasize a family, and that is unspoken expectations. God intended us to love and respect each other fully, as well as work as a team. By identifying our roles early and often we can avoid the fallout of unfulfilled and unspoken expectations. Prayerfully come together and create a plan of who does what.

REDISCOVERING INDEPENDENCE: *A FATHER'S NEW IDENTITY*

Sometimes, as fathers, we might catch ourselves worrying about losing our independence and individuality. It's a common concern, one that often brings stress and uncertainty. This fear can manifest in various aspects of our lives. As we juggle all our roles, we might feel that personal time, hobbies, and interests take a back seat. There's this nagging worry that we might not be the person we once were. Instead of being known for our unique traits, we fear being solely identified as "Ethan, Mason, Lawson, and Colton's dad," with little left of our own identity.

But what does God have to say about losing our independence?

> 1 Peter 2:16: "Live as free people, but do not use your freedom as a cover-up for evil; live as God's slaves."

> Galatians 5:13: "You, my brothers and sisters, were called to be free. But do not use your freedom to indulge the flesh; rather, serve one another humbly in love."

To truly understand these passages, we need to reconsider the ideas of freedom and independence. It's not just about the "self." God's view of our independence is much broader and deeper. It's more than just who we are as individuals, but how we live in God's grace. True Christian freedom means being liberated from the guilt of sin through Christ's forgiveness (Eph. 1:7; Rom. 8:1) and from the penalty of sin because of Christ's sacrifice (Rom. 5:8–10; 6:23). We are freed from the constraints and dangers of the law, and through God's Spirit, the power of sin over us is broken (Rom. 6:1–23; Heb. 2:14).

We were made in the image of God, and God has given us free will to live life according to the Word. By doing so we are saved and forgiven of our sins. We are no longer shackled by our shortcomings and sin. We are no longer slaves to sin and being condemned. We are saved in the eyes of our Lord. With this in mind, we can start to think of fatherhood as a kind of rediscovery of our independence—not a hindrance to it. We can even be excited to reshape our identity, not just as "dad," but as individuals living in God's grace.

For many dads, fatherhood feels like a slow-motion train wreck, careening toward the abyss of lost independence. We imagine ourselves defined solely by the number of kids clinging to our legs. We fear losing our passions, our very selves. But God doesn't see freedom the same way we do. He's not concerned with your ability to binge-watch Netflix without interruption. God's freedom is about liberation. You're a child of God, forgiven and redeemed. You're no longer shackled by the chains of your past. You're free to live, love, and raise your kids without the weight of sin on your shoulders.

Suddenly, fatherhood doesn't look so bad, does it? It isn't a prison; it's a chance to redefine yourself. It's an opportunity to be a role model, a teacher, a friend. Embrace the chaos. Dive headfirst into the sticky fingers and endless questions. Because in the midst of it all, you might just discover a new kind of freedom, a freedom that comes from love, purpose, and a deep connection to something bigger than yourself.

TOMORROW'S KEEPERS: *THE MAGIC OF PROACTIVE PARENTING*

The worry about our children's health and safety is a concern that quietly lingers in every father's heart. I've found that most dads, myself included, share a deep-seated fear of anything tragic befalling our kids. It's a thought so overwhelming that it's often hard to fully grasp.

Through the years, I've crossed paths with incredible men, many of whom I still consider friends, who have endured the heartbreak of losing a child. Take my friend, Mark. His journey through the loss of his fourteen-year-old daughter to cancer was a profound lesson in strength and love. I first met Mark on a

Zoom call for our mastermind group for dads. The rawness of his experience, as he shared it alongside his wife, Trish, was both heart-wrenching and deeply human. To witness the pain in his eyes, yet also the unyielding strength in his voice, was an unforgettable moment of shared grief and solidarity.

Another dear friend and business partner, Jason, faced a similar tragedy when he lost his nineteen-year-old daughter, Chloe, in a car accident. Walking alongside Jason in his journey of grief has been a poignant reminder of the fragility of life and the strength of fatherly love. These experiences, as harrowing as they are, underscore a fear that, while not always spoken, is ever-present in the hearts of dads like Mark, Jason, and myself.

Amidst these fears, the wisdom of the Bible offers a comforting perspective:

Proverbs 3:5–6: "Trust in the LORD with all your heart and lean not on your own understanding; in all your ways submit to him, and he will make your paths straight."

Psalm 55:22: "Cast your cares on the LORD and he will sustain you; he will never let the righteous be shaken."

Philippians 4:6–7: "Do not be anxious about anything, but in every situation, by prayer and petition, with thanksgiving, present your requests to God. And the peace of God, which transcends all understanding, will guard your hearts and your minds in Christ Jesus."

There is no promise of a life without health hardship. However, there is a promise a plan exists that is greater than our own. Proactively preparing our children for what could potentially happen means constantly checking in with who they are and where they are susceptible to possible dangers.

All fathers have the chance to lay down foundations of love, understanding, and courage in our kids—all of which will be a kind of force field as they face the hazards of life. The protection doesn't just mitigate our fears. It transforms those fears into actionable insights that will empower both us and our children over the long term. Proactive parenting, then, is essentially weaving a safety net of support that is as spiritual as it is emotional. It's about being there—and I mean *really* there—for our kids, teaching them to navigate life's complexities with grace and strength. Hopefully, with God as their guide, fears will eventually become less about what we could lose and more about what we all stand to gain from the unpredictable nature of the world.

Our role as tomorrow's keepers is not just about being a protector but protecting through a legacy of love, resilience, and faith.

LESSONS IN GRACE: *LEARNING FROM MEANINGFUL MISTAKES*

Talk to any dad out there, and they'll probably agree: messing up isn't on our list of favorite things to do, especially when it comes to our kids. What's even more challenging is when we find ourselves repeating the same mistakes, over and over again. Whether it's losing our temper, saying something we regret, or disappointing our kids, making mistakes is tough. But facing those repeated mishaps? That's even tougher.

When it comes to making mistakes, the Bible offers profound insights:

Romans 3:23: "For all have sinned and fall short of the glory of God."

1 John 1:9: "If we confess our sins, he is faithful and just and will forgive us our sins and purify us from all unrighteousness."

Psalm 103:13–14: "As a father has compassion on his children, so the LORD has compassion on those who fear him; for he knows how we are formed, he remembers that we are dust."

Spoiler alert: we're all human, and yes, that means mistakes are part of the package. More often than not, the hardest person to forgive, to offer a little grace to, is the guy looking back at us in the mirror. Consider how quickly God extends forgiveness when we ask with humble hearts. Also, think about how fast we forgive our children when they apologize. Yet, forgiving ourselves seems like a mountain too high to climb. We don't have to carry the burden of self-forgiveness when we make mistakes. Actually, it's the enemy who wants us burdened by this, making us feel unworthy of God's love. Let's not fall into this trap.

Every last one of us stumbles on the path to fatherhood. We trip over our shoelaces and land face-first in the mud. We forget lunchboxes and miss school plays. We blurt out things we don't mean. But here's the thing: those stumbles, those face-plants, those blunders? They're not the enemy. They're the map. Each stumble is a chance to learn, to grow, to become a better man. It's a chance to practice grace, not just for our kids, but for ourselves. What kind of hypocrite would we be if we taught our children the importance of humility, responsibility, and sincere apologies while we ourselves wallowed in self-doubt and shame?

Nobody expects you to be perfect. That's not the point. The point is to learn from your mistakes. They're the dues you pay on the path to becoming a better father, a better man. And let me tell you, the view from the top is worth the climb. So, dust yourself off, learn your lesson, and move on. And the next time you see your kid trip and fall, don't just pick them up. Kneel down beside them, look them in the eye, and say, "Hey, guess what? I fell down too once. But you know what? I got back up." You're not just a father. You're a teacher.

STRENGTH IN VULNERABILITY: *HAVING THE COURAGE TO BE SCARED*

Men are often indoctrinated from a young age, with society reinforcing the notion that feelings of sadness, fear, desperation, or even exhaustion are signs of weakness. We're told to "suck it up, buttercup!" and expected to never show signs of being weary, tired, sad, or scared. Many of us grew up in environments where expressing these feelings was frowned upon. These societal expectations are further amplified in adult relationships, at the workplace, and even on social media.

What God has to say about vulnerability:

2 Corinthians 12: 9–10: But he said to me, "My grace is sufficient for you, for my power is made perfect in weakness." Therefore I will boast all the more gladly about my weaknesses, so that Christ's power may rest on me. That is why, for Christ's sake, I delight in weaknesses, in insults, in hardships, in persecutions, in difficulties. For when I am weak, then I am strong.

When you ask most men, they'll admit that being vulnerable with anyone is a frightening prospect. There are countless reasons and stories we've convinced ourselves of to avoid showing the real us, hiding behind a façade of strength we prefer to present to the world. Consider how we typically respond to a simple "How are you?" Often, our automatic replies are "Good," "Fine," or "Busy," irrespective of the actual turmoil or stress we might be experiencing. We strive to maintain a veneer of being untroubled, unwilling to let our families see us in a moment of vulnerability or challenge.

Yet, in these moments of perceived weakness, God reminds us that true strength, courage, and relatability are revealed. Authenticity and vulnerability serve as the glue that holds relationships together. Being open and vulnerable during tough times signals trust and invites a deeper connection with those around us.

As fathers, we naturally want our kids to be open with us, to share their struggles and fears. We feel honored when our children trust us enough to talk about their challenges. To foster this level of openness consistently, we need to embody it ourselves. Again, the most impactful life lessons are often caught, not taught. We can encourage our kids to share their difficulties with us all we want, but if they don't see us practicing what we preach, it loses its power.

Every dad is terrified of messing up, of letting their kids down, of failing to live up to the impossible standards we set for ourselves. But here's the thing: those fears, those doubts, those anxieties are more Bat-Signal than Kryptonite. The more we hide our vulnerabilities, the more we teach our kids that strength means never showing weakness. We build this fortress of masculinity around ourselves, brick by brick, convinced that the only way to be a good father is to be a fearless one. True strength, however, comes from facing your fears head-on. It's about being honest with yourself and others about what scares you, hurts you, makes you cry. It's about showing your kids that it's just fine to feel the full spectrum of human emotions. When you do that, something magical happens. You tear down the walls and build bridges instead. You create a space where your kids feel safe to share their own vulnerabilities, where they know they're loved and accepted for who they are, not who they pretend to be.

Next time you feel the fear creeping in, don't push it away. Don't swallow it down and pretend it's not there. Talk about it. Share it. Let your kids see that their dad is also afraid sometimes. Vulnerability isn't weakness. It's the key to unlocking true strength, the kind that connects us to our loved ones, and, of course, our children.

CHAPTER II
A FATHER'S SPIRITUAL GROWTH

"Larry, have you embraced your identity in Christ as a husband and father?" This question, posed to me during a Bible study group with seven of my closest friends, all husbands and fathers, really struck a chord. Being candid, I didn't like the question, and I wasn't sure how to respond.

I felt an inner conflict as I pondered not just the answer, but the depth of the question itself. I had always seen my identity as something unique to me, not necessarily linked to my faith. The idea that God could be intertwined with my many roles hadn't really crossed my mind before. It wasn't that I was opposed to the idea; it simply hadn't occurred to me.

Now, confronted with this thought, I felt a bit foolish for not even thinking of the concept on my own. Did I overlook something in the past we had studied? Did I miss something in the Bible? Did I even deserve to have an identity in Christ as a man, husband, father, and human being? I admit, I'm still quite new to all of this. The deepening of my relationship with Christ only began in 2020. So, I am still studying and growing. It's a significant learning curve, but also an incredibly enriching experience. It challenges me to question the norm and pushes me to grow spiritually.

This journey of seeking and embracing our identity in Christ is deeply personal and spiritual. I encourage everyone to embark on a similar quest. It involves a profound exploration of who we are in the context of our faith and how this shapes us in our roles as fathers. It's about understanding and accepting our place in God's plan and letting that guide us in our daily lives.

Early on, I learned the real transformation fathers undergo is spiritual. It's a crash course in humility, a baptism by fire in patience, and a masterclass in love that transcends logic. You learn to see the world through eyes filled with wonder, to find joy in the mundane, and to sacrifice your own needs for the sake of another. Fatherhood isn't a walk in the park; it's a boot camp for the soul, one that leaves you hardened in resilience, softened in compassion, and ultimately, closer to the divine than you ever thought possible.

SOULFUL REFLECTION: *DISCOVERING YOUR SPIRITUAL IDENTITY AS A DAD*

Embarking on a journey of spiritual growth as a father often starts with regular Bible study. For Christians, the Bible offers guidance on living a life centered in faith. Take, for example, 2 Corinthians 5:17 ("Therefore, if anyone is in Christ, the new creation has come: The old has gone, the new is here!"), which reveals the transformative power of Christ. However, approaching the Bible can be overwhelming, especially when done in isolation. It's important to understand why this is a challenge in order to make Bible study more accessible and meaningful for all of us. One major hurdle is the complex language and style of the Bible. Especially in certain translations, it uses archaic language and a literary style that can be challenging for modern readers. This complexity creates a barrier, particularly for those who are not familiar with historical or biblical terminology. Additionally, the cultural and historical context of the Bible, written in different times and places, can make it difficult for readers to relate to its stories, language, and references. Understanding the context of specific passages, including their historical, cultural, and theological background, is crucial for proper interpretation. Without this context, it's tough to fully grasp the intended meaning.

Moreover, the Bible's length and diversity of content can be daunting. It encompasses a wide range of genres, including history, poetry, prophecy, and letters, which can overwhelm, especially those new to the text. Each literary genre within the Bible requires a different approach for interpretation, which only adds to the challenge. Personal beliefs and expectations also play a significant role in how people approach the Bible. Preexisting beliefs and worldviews can influence the interpretation of and reaction to biblical passages. Some individuals may also struggle with seeing the relevance of biblical teachings in their daily lives. They may find it hard to connect these ancient texts with their contemporary concerns and challenges.

Another factor is limited biblical literacy. A lack of familiarity with biblical stories, characters, and themes can make it difficult for readers to understand the references and allusions within the text. Moreover, the sacredness of the Bible can instill a fear of misinterpretation or misunderstanding in readers, creating a barrier to deeper engagement. Furthermore, many people lead busy lives, making it challenging to find time for consistent, focused Bible reading. This busyness and the distractions of daily life can affect the ability to engage deeply with the text. To overcome these challenges, individuals may find it beneficial to utilize study tools, select a translation that suits their reading style, seek guidance from pastors or mentors, participate in group studies, and approach the Bible with an open mind and a willingness to thoughtfully explore its messages.

I can personally attest to feeling intimidated when I first started reading the Bible. My initial attempts left me confused and doubting my ability to understand scripture. I often felt unworthy of even trying to forge a deeper connection with God, thinking that my struggles with the Bible were transparent to the Divine. However, with time,

I came to see the Bible as an invaluable source of truth and clarity on topics that often leave us with more questions than answers.

A significant turning point for me, and many others, was realizing that this journey was not meant to be a solitary endeavor. Joining a group on this spiritual path proved to be a game changer. Regular Bible studies and learning from those more knowledgeable about scripture provided immense reassurance and support. It became clear that studying the Bible shouldn't be a solitary pursuit. Finding a community, especially those who are further along in their spiritual journey, can offer invaluable insights and guidance.

The journey of spiritual growth as a father can start with Bible study, but it is enriched and deepened by sharing the journey with others. Remember, having a group to share your spiritual life with is transformative in your path as a father.

PRAYERFUL BONDING: *HARNESSING THE STRENGTH OF DIVINE COMMUNICATION*

Prayer serves as our sacred means to communicate with God, allowing us to seek guidance and gain deeper understanding. It's not just about asking for things; it's also about listening to God's voice, which fosters a more profound relationship with the Divine. My own journey with prayer was marked by uncertainty in the beginning. I often approached God merely seeking assistance or guidance through crises, not realizing the full potential of prayer.

A few years ago, a spiritual mentor introduced me to the "ACTS" method of prayer, which profoundly changed my approach. The first part, *Adoration*, is a time to express our love and reverence for God, acknowledging what has been done for us. Psalm 100:5 beautifully guides us in this: "For the Lord is good and his love endures forever; his faithfulness continues through all generations." Even Jesus taught His followers to start their prayers with adoration, saying, "Our Father in heaven, hallowed be your name" (Matt. 6:9). Sometimes, I find solace in this scripture, but at other times, I simply express my love for God in my own words.

Then comes *Confession*, which involves admitting our sins to God. This can be a difficult step, as it often brings feelings of shame and guilt. Psalm 32:3–5 shows us David's approach to confession: "When I kept silent [about my sin], my bones wasted away through my groaning all day long. For day and night your hand was heavy upon me; my strength was sapped as in the heat of summer. Then I acknowledged my sin to you and did not cover up my iniquity. I said, 'I will confess my wrong-doings to the LORD.' And you forgave the guilt of my sin." It reminds us that although God is aware of our sins, confessing them signifies our acknowl-edgment of their offensiveness and our need for Jesus's cleansing from unrighteousness.

Thanksgiving in prayer isn't limited to times of joy and prosperity. Scripture encourages us to main-tain gratitude that most of us don't realize. It's easy to be grateful in the seasons when everything is going exceptionally well. However, being grateful for difficulties can be extremely challenging. I know it sounds odd, but even our suffering is something we can look at through the lens of appreciation. Most of us have been through seasons of challenge or even seasons that we didn't think we could make it out of such darkness. However, the difficult times often serve as the backdrop for God's most profound work in our lives, turning our trials into blessings. This perspective on gratitude helps us recognize that even in our darkest moments, God is working for us, not against us.

Lastly, *Supplication* is about making our requests known to God. As Jesus said in Matthew 7:7–8, "Ask, and it will be given to you; seek and you will find; knock and the door will be opened to you. For everyone who asks receives; the one who seeks finds; and to the one who knocks, the door will be opened." This is not to say that all our requests will be given to us. It's no different than when our kids ask us for things we know will not serve them. When it comes to our children, sometimes the answer must be no. It's no different than our relationship with God, who has a plan for us and will not give us everything we want or ask for.

Before learning this method, my relationship with God felt one-dimensional, often resembling a child who turns to his father only when in need. Discovering the ACTS framework revolutionized my prayer life, providing a structured yet intimate way to converse with God. I've also incorporated moments of silence into my prayer routine, allowing space to listen to what God might be teaching me.

Sharing this framework with my children has not only nurtured their faith but also equipped them with a way to communicate with God that feels personal and unburdened.

THE FORGIVENESS TRAIL: *LETTING GO TO MOVE FORWARD*

Embracing forgiveness is a journey that unfolds in three distinct ways. When we think of forgiveness, it's often about the wrongs others have done to us. This is indeed an important aspect, but there's more to the forgiveness process than what initially meets the eye.

First, recognizing that we are beloved children of God is essential. It's a comforting realization to know we are loved by such a merciful and forgiving Heavenly Father. Secondly, we must extend forgiveness to others who have wronged, hurt, or betrayed us. This act of forgiving is not just for their benefit but ours as well. God teaches us that holding onto grudges harms us more than the offender. Ephesians 4:31–32 guides us in this: "Get rid of all bitterness, rage and anger, brawling and slander, along with every form of malice. Be kind and compassionate to one another, forgiving each other, just as in Christ God forgave you." This passage encourages us to let go of negative emotions and embrace forgiveness, mirroring the forgiveness God grants us through Jesus Christ.

Colossians 3:13 reiterates this message: "Bear with each other and forgive one another if any of you has a grievance against someone. Forgive as the Lord forgave you." Like Ephesians, Colossians emphasizes the need to forgive and underscores the importance of forgiving others as a reflection of how the Lord forgave us.

Luke 6:37 adds: "Do not judge, and you will not be judged. Do not condemn, and you will not be condemned. Forgive, and you will be forgiven." This verse links our forgiveness of others to how we are treated by God, emphasizing a reciprocal relationship in mercy.

Finally, self-forgiveness for our own mistakes, shortcomings, and wrongdoings is crucial. Often, the most challenging forgiveness is forgiving ourselves. Many men I've worked with find it hardest to forgive the person they see in the mirror. We must remember that God didn't create us on this earth to live a mediocre life and carry the burden of constant guilt and shame. He wants us to live life fully, and clinging to these negative feelings only impedes our spiritual journey. Being able to ask for forgiveness is a liberating process.

Scriptures like 1 John 1:9 remind us of this: "If we confess our sins, he is faithful and just and will forgive us our sins and purify us from all unrighteousness." This verse emphasizes the importance of confessing our sins and embracing God's forgiveness.

Romans 8:1 further assures us: "Therefore, there is now no condemnation for those who are in Christ Jesus." This verse highlights the freedom from guilt and shame that comes through a relationship with Jesus.

Psalm 103:12 beautifully illustrates the completeness of God's forgiveness: "As far as the east is from the west, so far has he removed our transgressions from us." God completely removes our sins and if God doesn't hold our sins against us, we should not continue to hold them against ourselves either.

Finally, Isaiah 43:25 states: "I, even I, am he who blots out your transgressions, for my own sake, and remembers your sins no more." This verse reinforces the concept of God's total forgiveness, encouraging us to release ourselves from past burdens.

Forgiveness involves understanding God's merciful nature, extending forgiveness to others, and importantly, forgiving ourselves. This path of forgiveness is crucial for moving forward, unshackled by past grievances, and stepping into the fullness of life with God.

THE PRACTICE OF RECONCILIATION: *PRACTICAL STEPS IN FORGIVENESS*

Forgiveness: it's a powerful force in the complex web of our relationships. It goes beyond just letting someone off the hook; it's like offering a heartfelt gift. It's not only beneficial for the person who's forgiven; it's surprisingly healing for the one who forgives, as well.

Think of forgiveness as more than a simple "everything is okay." It's about choosing not to lug around those heavy feelings of anger or hurt anymore. When you forgive, it's not solely for the other person's benefit; it's about giving yourself a break too. It's like clearing out the old, negative baggage to make space for positive, uplifting experiences.

So, in essence, forgiving isn't just an act of kindness toward others; it's a self-care act, enriching your life by deciding to step away from the past and stride toward a more joyful future.

Holding a grudge is like you drinking poison and waiting for the other person to die. Picture clinging to a grudge as if it were a bottle of hemlock. You take a sip, expecting the other person to feel the pain. In truth, clinging to a grudge is more like poisoning yourself while hoping the other person suffers. The bitterness and resentment erode your own happiness, impacting your emotions and mindset. The other person might not even realize the turmoil you're in, leaving you alone to deal with the harmful effects. This metaphor really drives home the self-destructive nature of resentment, emphasizing that letting go is not just a kindness to others but a vital act of self-care and emotional well-being.

Now, for some practical steps to help you overcome any residual anger you might be feeling after an argument. First, you need to acknowledge your emotions and talk about how you feel. Just pause for a moment and think of what went down. We all say things we don't mean, which, unfortunately, can slip out and hurt another's feelings without us realizing what has happened. Getting everything out in the open is not only a great idea—it has some real emotional benefits.

Try and imagine you are the other person. Not that we should excuse what they did, but sometimes when you really understand the other person's point of view it can help make forgiveness easier. When you are ready, make the decision to forgive. But don't just tell the other person. Show your forgiveness if you can manage it. The main thing is to release any and all negative vibes. It may take time, but true forgiveness is essential. Concentrate on the present and the future. Focus on the positive in your life and your relationships. And don't forget to be gentle with yourself through all of this. While forgiving might be shockingly hard, it demonstrates real bravery and marks the beginning of a new chapter with the person you are upset with.

One year, around Christmas, we were packing up the car with the kids, gifts, and food to head over to my dad's house for the holidays. My second oldest son, who was fifteen years old at the time, was helping me. After packing up the car, he looked me right in the eyes with all sincerity and asked: "Can I ask you something?"

I knew a big question was coming because he always has the same look when he is about to drop a question on me that has been stewing for a long time.

"Of course." I replied.

"Do you like going over to your dad's house? Do you like being there?"

I smiled because I knew that this question came from the deepest part of his heart and there was more to this question than met the eye.

I warmly smiled, "Mason, why do you ask?"

"Dad, I don't know how you like going over there. I enjoy being over there because they are nice, and we all get along well. But I always wonder how you do it? He left you not once but twice." He paused and really discerned what he said next.

"I could never forgive you . . . never. If you left, it would hurt me so much that I would never be able to forgive you and I wouldn't want you in my life."

I shook my head and warmly smiled. I can always appreciate Mason's honesty. He only says something like this when he truly believes it to his core.

My mind raced to give him the best answer I could. This was an important question and one of those moments as a dad that you want to give the best explanation possible.

My mom and biological father were married young at the age of twenty-one. They had me a few years later in 1975. When I was around one, my mother and father divorced. He left, and I had no recollection of my biological father. When I was five, my mom remarried, my stepfather adopted me, and I assumed his name. When that marriage fell apart, I was ten years old. I started asking my mom about my natural father and at the age of twelve he came back into my life. He was remarried with a two-year-old son and another son on the way. Our reunion was unplanned but welcomed. I spent time with him and his family. He came to my little league games, took me to do fun things, and I enjoyed every minute we had together. After about six months of us spending time together, I noticed a change in our connection and just like that, we parted ways.

In 2005 something unexpected happened. I was in a coffee shop in St. Louis when I noticed a man walk through the door to get his morning coffee. I couldn't believe what I was seeing. I hadn't seen my father since I was twelve years old. That unexpected encounter has turned into a nearly twenty-year relationship. He is still married to the same wonderful woman, and I have two younger half brothers. Our families spend time together often and my boys know them well. We have had a few conversations about the past and what has transpired. My dad has owned every decision he made, and I have forgiven him.

"I understand that and to be honest there is a part of me that feels that way too. However, my dad has apologized and asked for forgiveness. I have given him that forgiveness. I have given him grace not just for him, but for me too."

"What do you mean?" he asked.

"There was once a part of me that felt justified to be angry and hold a grudge against my dad. There was once a part of me that felt I should somehow punish my dad for the choices he has made. However, truly, I tell you, that doesn't do him or me any favors. In fact, the person it harms the most is me."

"I don't understand," he said curiously.

"Mason, holding a grudge against my dad or anyone is like me drinking poison and hoping the other person will die. The person who harbors the grudge is the one who carries the heaviest burden. My heavenly Father forgives my sins every single time I sin, and that grace is always available to me.

As you get older, there will be things you might feel anger at toward me because of mistakes I have or will make with you. I can only hope you show me the same grace. We are all human and we will all make mistakes. Some are big and some are small. We are taught to forgive and love as Christ did. My dad is seventy-five years old, and I don't know how much more time I have with him. I am not going to waste our time or connection by holding a grudge that tears our relationship apart."

I saw a sense of calm wash over Mason's face as if he started to understand the importance of forgiveness, which is a powerful leadership quality that will not only improve our own lives but also elevate the quality of our kids' lives.

IDENTITY REDISCOVERED: *NURTURING THE SOUL OF A FATHER*

In the midst of the journey of rediscovering our identity as fathers, nurturing our souls becomes paramount. This aligns closely with the fruits of the Spirit listed in Galatians 5:22–23, which includes love, joy, peace, patience, kindness, goodness, faithfulness, gentleness, and self-control.

These qualities, reflecting the character of Christ, serve as essential benchmarks for our personal and spiritual development. I have often found in my life that when things seem off-kilter, it's usually because one or more of these fruits are lacking. For instance, if my relationship with one of my sons feels tense, I reflect on whether I am embodying patience, kindness, or joy in our interactions. If my health and fitness goals are not being met, it might be due to a lapse in self-control. And when things feel strained with my wife, Jess, it's often a sign that I need to focus more on being gentle, kind, or maintaining a more joyful spirit. These fruits of the Spirit act as guardrails, helping to guide our actions and decisions, particularly in our roles as fathers.

However, cultivating these qualities is just the beginning of the process. It's through our unwavering commitment to spiritual disciplines that these traits truly flourish. In life, the areas we focus on and commit to are the ones that grow and prosper. If we neglect attending weekly church services, or if we aren't engaging with the Bible regularly, our faith may start to flounder. The same goes for skipping our weekly Bible study groups or not maintaining the practice of praying at the dinner table with our families or before bed. Such practices are crucial in keeping our faith, and that of our families, strong and vibrant.

Embracing our identity in Christ is rooted in a daily regimen of living within specific spiritual guardrails. Many of us try to navigate this on our own and end up feeling lost and alone. But by actively practicing our faith through regular scripture reading, prayer, engaging in community, seeking guidance and mentorship, practicing forgiveness and humility, and demonstrating leadership, we can more readily embrace our identity in Christ.

These practices are integral to shaping our identity, not just as men or believers, but specifically as fathers. Deepen your connection with God and, through this, enrich the lives of those you love and lead. Embrace the vulnerability required to nurture your soul and cultivate those fruits of the Spirit. Immerse yourself in the spiritual disciplines that nourish your faith and seek guidance and support from other men walking the same path. As you do, you'll find that your identity as a father becomes a powerful force for good, shaping not just your own life but the lives of your children and the world around you.

THE IMPERFECT PARENT: *CELEBRATING OUR UNIQUENESS*

Imposter syndrome is a stealthy intruder that often sneaks into the minds and hearts of even the most accomplished individuals—parents included. It's usually a voice of self-doubt, one that is critical, dismissing our achievements and capabilities despite clear evidence of our competence and success. The resulting psychological pattern leaves us feeling like frauds, undeserving of the success we've achieved. It can also hinder our future success and personal fulfillment, since, at its core, there is an underlying belief that we are, quite simply, not worthy. We doubt our abilities and fear being exposed as undeserving of our current position, title, relationship, level of economic status, and even faith.

In my work, I've encountered men who manage multimillion-dollar companies, maintain excellent physical fitness, have beautiful homes, cars, and families, and still believe they don't deserve any of it. They fear it might all be taken away because they were never deserving in the first place. Even some of the most well-known people I've interviewed (whose names I'll keep confidential) have expressed uncertainty about how they've attained their level of status.

Personally, I've grappled with imposter syndrome throughout my life. Since I was young, I viewed my future as bleak, or if I did achieve success, I was paranoid that I wasn't deserving of it. We all experience times when the voice of imposter syndrome is overwhelmingly loud and other times when it's just a whisper. But for most of us, it's always there to some degree.

The voice of imposter syndrome is a tool the enemy uses against us. Why else would we talk so poorly about ourselves and create a scarcity mindset that steals the joy of our current success, no matter its level? We're plagued by whispers like, "You aren't good enough at your job, and your boss will find out," or "You don't deserve your loving spouse," or "You aren't a good enough parent."

God, who loves us more than we can imagine, would never want us or our children to endure this inner dialogue. Thus, we should recognize that the feelings and self-talk of imposter syndrome will keep us from reaching our best potential.

We must remember that prayer is a two-way street of communication. In Matthew 11:28–29,

Jesus invites us to find rest in Him, saying, "Come to me, all you who are weary and burdened, and I will give you rest. Take my yoke upon you and learn from me, for I am gentle and humble in heart, and you will find rest for your souls." God knows our feelings of imposter syndrome and inadequacy and doesn't want us to live burdened by these thoughts, as they steal our joy, fulfillment, and the ability for us to do good.

Embracing our uniqueness as parents is key to overcoming the crippling self-doubt of imposter syndrome. If you celebrate the individuality and distinct contributions you make to your family, you should be able to break free from the shackles of self-imposed inadequacy, and fully step into your role as dad, loved and guided by a God who values you for who you are.

PROGRESS OVER PERFECTION: *EMBRACING THE JOURNEY OF PERSONAL GROWTH*

The thief of our joy is often comparison and the misguided belief that perfection is within reach. I am a strong advocate for striving for success in all aspects of life, including parenting, marriage, leadership, fitness, faith, finances, and business. However, for us to relish the journey and prevent imposter syndrome from sneaking in, setting achievable goals is essential.

In a world brimming with polished social media profiles and success stories that frequently skip life's hardships, it's easy to fall into the trap of comparison. This can rob us of the joy found in our unique journey. As we experience life's complexities—parenting, marriage, leadership, and beyond—choosing progress over perfection becomes a freeing mantra. The quest for perfection, often an unattainable illusion, can impede our ability to cherish the small advancements that constitute our personal and professional growth. Real success is not in the unachievable perfection but in the tangible progress we make, step by step.

Setting attainable goals is not about settling but about choosing a mindset of continual improvement. The quest for perfection can breed anxiety, creating a culture of self-doubt and imposter syndrome. By shifting our focus to attainable goals, we allow ourselves to experiment, learn, and adapt. In the intricate tapestry of life's pursuits, understanding that progress is dynamic lets us celebrate even the smallest victories, which are often overshadowed by the pursuit of an idealized end state. It's important to recognize that the path to success is rarely a straight line. It's full of obstacles, adversity, frustrations, and setbacks. Keeping imposter syndrome at bay means accepting this as part of our journey.

Each detour, rather than being a failure, is a valuable lesson that propels us toward personal and professional growth. The apparent steps back offer a chance to reassess our strategies, hone our skills, and fortify our resilience. By understanding that setbacks are not roadblocks but stepping stones, we transform adversity into an ally. This mindset enables us to face challenges with an unwavering sense of determination.

The unpredictability of our journey adds richness and texture to our experiences. Challenges reveal our true strengths and endurance. While daunting, the twists and turns of our path are full of adventure and discovery. Only by navigating through uncharted territories can we uncover the hidden aspects of our character. This understanding liberates us from unrealistic expectations, allowing us to appreciate the goals right there in front of us.

Philippians 3:12–14 beautifully captures this sentiment: "Not that I have already obtained all this, or have already arrived at my goal, but I press on to take hold of that for which Christ Jesus took hold of me. Brothers and sisters, I do not consider myself yet to have taken hold of it. But one thing I do: Forgetting what is behind and straining toward what is ahead, I press on toward the goal to win the prize for which God has called me heavenward in Christ Jesus."

In this passage, the Apostle Paul highlights the ongoing nature of striving toward goals, acknowledging his path toward spiritual growth. He begins by admitting that he has not yet achieved spiritual perfection or fully reached his goal. His humility is significant, reflecting an understanding that spiritual maturity is a continuous practice, not a final destination.

Despite not having reached the ultimate goal, Paul's resolve to press on is unwavering. He is driven by the purpose for which Christ took hold of him, encompassing living by Christ's teachings, spreading the gospel, and growing in spiritual maturity.

Paul emphasizes the importance of not dwelling on past achievements or failures. He acknowledges his past but chooses not to be defined or constrained by it.

This forward-looking perspective encourages believers to concentrate on the present and future, rather than being weighed down by past successes or mistakes.

The phrase "straining toward what is ahead" suggests intense effort and focus. Paul urges believers to dedicate themselves to their spiritual journey, directing their energy toward the continuous pursuit of a deeper relationship with Christ.

The "goal" Paul refers to is the prize for which believers strive. This prize, described as the ultimate calling heavenward in Christ Jesus, likely includes the reward of eternal life and fulfilling God's purpose for each individual. So, while perfection is an unreachable illusion, setting realistic goals and embracing every aspect of our journey, including its setbacks and triumphs, is where true fulfillment and joy lie.

This mindset not only leads to more successful outcomes, but also enriches our lives with continuous learning, growth, and satisfaction.

GOALS WITHIN REACH: *SETTING REALISTIC EXPECTATIONS*

The journey of a father is one filled with a spectrum of emotions—it's enjoyable, humbling, exciting, but also frustrating and at times, quite devastating. The key to maximizing the fulfillment and minimizing those crushing moments lies in setting realistic goals and expectations. Together, they form both the foundation and launching point of being a productive dad.

From the beginning, it's important to reflect on your values. As a Christian father, identifying your core beliefs is paramount. Ask yourself, what principles and virtues do you wish to instill in your children? Understanding and embracing your values will guide you in setting expectations that resonate with your faith.

Assessing your abilities and limitations is another vital step. Being honest with yourself about your strengths and weaknesses as a father is crucial. Recognizing that no one is perfect and that it's okay to have limitations is part of this self-awareness. Identifying areas where you might need improvement can help in formulating more realistic expectations.

Life is inherently unpredictable, filled with unexpected challenges and changes. This requires a degree of flexibility and the ability to adapt your expectations as circumstances evolve. Being flexible is an important quality for any parent, helping you navigate through the ups and downs of family life. Seeking wise counsel is also highly beneficial. Consulting with other Christian fathers or mentors who have experience in parenting can offer valuable insights and guidance. Their experiences and perspectives can be instrumental in helping you set realistic and attainable expectations for your parenting journey.

A critical aspect of setting realistic expectations is to avoid comparisons. Every family is unique, and what works for one may not necessarily work for another. Instead of comparing your family or parenting style to others, focus on your family's individual needs and circumstances. This will help in tailoring your goals and expectations to suit your family's unique dynamics.

Lastly, practicing self-care is essential. Taking care of your physical, mental, and spiritual well-being enables you to be the best version of yourself for your family. When you are well-rested and in a balanced state, you're better equipped to meet your family's needs and set realistic expectations.

Fathers need to forget what they've heard about setting goals being some grueling, self-flagellating ritual. It's not about beating yourself up over missed gym sessions or unrealized dreams. It's about under-standing what you can realistically achieve, adapting to the unexpected, borrowing wisdom from fellow dads, and, most importantly, not falling prey to the comparison game. It's about finding that sweet spot where ambition meets self-compassion. And when you do, setting goals doesn't feel like a chore, it feels like second nature. It becomes the fuel that propels you forward, not just as a father, but in all aspects of your life.

THE FATHERHOOD TRIBE: *FINDING YOUR COMMUNITY OF ENCOURAGEMENT*

Fatherhood can feel lonely at times, if not most of the time. When we step into this role, we often find ourselves withdrawing inward, isolating from the wider world. Our lives seem to revolve around just two primary spaces: work and family. In this new reality, our self-care and relationships, especially with friends, tend to take a backseat. Most of these external connections pause or stop altogether, usu-ally because we feel guilty spending time away from providing for our family at work or investing our physical, mental, emotional, and spiritual energy into our home life.

However, this isolation contrasts with the example set by Jesus, who often gathered disciples and followers around Him, forming a close-knit community. He emphasized the importance of relationships and mutual support. In Matthew 18:20, Jesus says, "For where two or three gather in my name, there am I with them." This verse underscores the significance of coming together in fellowship and community, a principle that is vital for fathers as well.

By actively participating in a community, we can lean into our support when things get difficult and frustrating in our lives. Through this support, we can more effectively navigate the challenges of fatherhood. These seasons of challenge become shorter, and we can return to a state of joy and fulfillment more quickly.

A community fulfills many human needs, like growth, curiosity, self-actualization, adaptability, competition, achievement, cognitive development, purpose, empathy, and many more. There is something incredibly powerful that happens when dads come together to support each other, elevate one another, and respectfully challenge each other to grow. In the Fatherhood Tribe, we share our strengths and experiences, shortening our learning curves through life's most challenging seasons by leveraging the crowd-sourced wisdom of like-minded men.

A Fatherhood Tribe will help balance your roles while nurturing our own growth and well-being. It's an incredible testament to the strength found in true fellowship and camaraderie, and a means to breaking the cycle of isolation in order to embrace the power of community. We will share our wisdom and experiences, shortening our learning curves and navigating life's challenges with the collective strength of our brotherhood.

HEART-LED LEADERSHIP: *PUTTING FAMILY AT THE FOREFRONT*

All too often, learning to be an effective leader is relegated to the sidelines in our lives. Yet, embracing this pivotal role is essential, and if we are unsure how to lead effectively, it's our duty to learn and grow in this area.

Many of us might have grown up with the misconception that leadership is about having the most dominant voice, controlling situations, or making unilateral decisions. This notion of leadership, often seen as dictatorial, can lead to environments filled with tension and discomfort. The essence of true leadership, however, especially in a family setting, is quite the opposite. Effective leadership isn't about being the loudest or most controlling person. A heart-led leader is one who nurtures and uplifts others. This leader leads by example, radiating compassion and empathy. This leader creates opportunities for meaningful conversations, ensuring every family member feels seen, heard, and safe. This leader listens more than speaks, actively engages in family life, and supports interests, hobbies, and passions. That doesn't mean sacrificing their own pursuits; rather, it's about balancing interests with those of the family, demonstrating that both can be valued and pursued harmoniously.

In the context of spiritual leadership, as stated in the phrase, "Put God first, then marriage, then kids," a heart-led father builds his family on a foundation deeply rooted in faith. Prioritizing God establishes a set of shared values and beliefs that guide family members in their decisions and behaviors, providing a moral compass for ethical choices and life's challenges.

Embracing God first in family life transcends mere adherence to religious norms; it's about nurturing a dynamic, living relationship with the Divine. As a spiritual leader, this means consistently seeking God's wisdom and guidance through prayer, engaging with sacred texts, and cultivating an environment conducive to spiritual growth. This approach not only shapes individual character but also fosters a collective spirit within the family, marked by love, kindness, and resilience amidst life's uncertainties. When God is at the heart of the family, faith becomes a tangible experience, influencing interactions and responses to life's challenges.

Furthermore, centering family life around shared faith serves as a steadfast anchor in both good times and bad. This shared faith becomes a source of strength, comfort, and unity, enabling the family to express collective gratitude in joyous times and find solace and hope during adversity. This foundational faith is not just for the present but is a legacy that influences generations, shaping the family's identity and approach to life's complexities.

When a family operates with this framework, decisions are more likely to be made through a Christian lens, enhancing the odds of making choices that are in line with shared values. Prioritizing faith within the family can be a unifying force, fostering a sense of belonging, purpose, and harmony. This approach helps family members feel more connected, both to each other and to a greater purpose. God wants us to grow spiritually as a family unit. In order to grow spiritually a foundation is essential. Without this unified force, spiritual growth can become more difficult to cultivate.

THE LANGUAGE OF LOVE: *AFFECTION BEYOND WORDS*

To love someone unconditionally is to love them without expecting anything in return. It's a selfless act of love that asks for nothing more than for the other person to simply be themselves. One of the most poignant verses that capture this essence is from 1 Corinthians 13:4–7: "Love is patient, love is kind. It does not envy, it does not boast, it is not proud. It does not dishonor others, it is not self-seeking, it is not easily angered, it keeps no record of wrongs. Love does not delight in evil but rejoices with the truth. It always protects, always trusts, always hopes, always perseveres."

For many of us, this can be challenging. We often love with conditions, saying we love someone unconditionally, but when wrongdoings occur or we are offended, our love can waver. This is particularly noticeable in marriages, where love can sometimes be conditional.

However, loving unconditionally doesn't mean allowing oneself to be disrespected or underappreciated. It involves communicating our needs without harboring ill will or resentment. Effective communication in a relationship acts as a bridge that connects us, and if our love is patient and kind, as described in 1 Corinthians, our communication should mirror these qualities.

The journey to love someone without conditions is a path of deep acceptance and understanding. As the Bible verse highlights, loving with patience, kindness, and forgiveness is ideal. In reality, though, life brings challenges and disagreements. Loving unconditionally teaches us not to ignore these difficulties but to view them as opportunities to grow and deepen our connection. It shows us that love's strength shines brightest not in perfection, but in the resilience to build a lasting bond despite imperfections.

In relationships, we often expect certain things in return for our love, especially in marriages. But unconditional love is not about ignoring these expectations; it's about committing to understand and grow through them. It asks us to face the ups and downs of love with unwavering acceptance of each other. Amidst the complexities of emotions, unconditional love acts as a constant thread, helping us to truly understand where our feelings stem from and thereby building a love that strengthens with every shared experience.

There will indeed be challenging times in our relationships, with misunderstandings along the way. However, if we continuously build our connection based on protection, trust, and hope through Christ, we will greatly enhance our chances of our love enduring. This is affection beyond words, where love is not just expressed in spoken language but demonstrated through actions and understanding, creating a bond that is fortified by faith and a genuine, heartfelt connection.

In the journey of loving someone unconditionally, we embark on a path of spiritual growth. The
essence of unconditional love, as beautifully articu-
lated in 1 Corinthians 13:4–7, reflects spiritual virtues such as patience, kindness, and forgiveness. As
we navigate the challenges and disagreements inherent in relationships, embracing unconditional love
becomes a profound act of spiritual acceptance and
understanding.

This path calls for a commitment to facing difficulties with unwavering acceptance, using them
as opportunities to grow and deepen our connection. The strength of unconditional love is not
found in perfection but in the resilience to build
lasting bonds despite imperfections. It teaches us to
view life's challenges as stepping stones to spiritual
growth, reinforcing our connection through protection, trust, and hope anchored in our faith.

Ultimately, unconditional love transcends mere
words; it is a demonstration of faith and a genuine,
heartfelt connection. By continuously building our
relationships on the foundation of protection, trust,
and hope through Christ, we not only enhance the
endurance of our love but also experience profound

spiritual growth, solidifying our connection on a deeper, more meaningful level.

KINDNESS IN MOTION: *LOVE AS A DAILY PRACTICE*

Over the years, listening to the stories of thousands of marriages, I've come across experiences of darkness, triumph, happiness, grief, joy, and conflict. A common thread that weaves through many of these relationships is a sense of lost love. Often, one or both partners express, "I don't know if I am in love with him/her anymore. The feeling of being in love is no longer there." This sentiment is a powerful reminder that the feeling of love can ebb and flow in.

From these myriad stories, including my own experiences in marriage, we learn that love's initial intensity can fade, leaving a void that often gets mistaken for the end of love. But perhaps this shift is a sign, an invitation to a deeper understanding that love is not just a fleeting feeling. It's a powerful force that can withstand the test of time, transforming and growing as couples navigate life together.

Often, we mistake love as merely a feeling that should persist effortlessly, especially after the honeymoon stage. But the truth is, love is an action as much as it is a feeling. When the euphoric feelings of love start to wane, it's not always a sign of love diminishing, but sometimes, it reflects our complacency and passivity in expressing love through our actions.

Reflecting on this brings to mind one of my favorite passages: "Dear children, let us not love with words or speech but with actions and in truth" (1 John 3:18). This verse beautifully encapsulates the essence of love as an active force. When we commit to loving our family through selfless actions, the feeling of love often naturally accompanies these actions. It's a daily practice of kindness, a demonstration that love extends beyond words.

In my personal journey with Jessica, spanning twenty-seven years of knowing each other and twenty years of marriage as of 2023, we've experienced our share of challenges. In the first half of our relationship, we both felt frustration and a lack of fulfillment, expecting that the feelings of "being in love" would always be present without the work of showing the other person how much we actually loved the other. At the start of our relationship, things felt easy, almost effortless. We were drawn to each other, both physically and emotionally. Overlooking flaws and quirks came naturally. In my eyes, she could do no wrong. In her eyes, I could do no wrong. However, over time, that initial "feeling" of love felt a shift. The once charming habits become bothersome, and the effortless feeling of love seemed harder to come by than in those early days.

It is natural that the "feeling of love" will ebb, particularly if we're not actively loving the other person. If we just wait for that sensation, without taking action, we risk being unfulfilled. Love isn't just an emotion that happens to us; it's an action, a choice. When we put effort into loving gestures, kind words, or spending quality time, we nurture a love that's not just felt but actively lived and experienced.

This paradox became clear to us over time: waiting for the feeling of love to reignite, without doing anything, is like expecting a garden to bloom without tending to it. Love needs nurturing, care, and attention. Understanding that love is an active verb, not just a passive sentiment, has been key for us. It's about breaking free from the cycle of waiting and stepping into a more proactive, vibrant connection. Through open and intentional communication, Jess and I have really dug into what makes us feel seen, loved, appreciated, and respected. For instance, leaving a note on her bathroom mirror that reads: "Good morning, lovely! I just want to let you know how much I appreciate all you do for us, and I love the way you love us. You are always so selfless, and you are always thinking about others. Plus, you are so unbelievably beautiful. I am honored to be the one to do life with you. Love you!—Me." makes a huge difference. It's these small acts, these moments of acknowledgment, that keep our love alive and thriving.

In the fabric of a strong and connected relationship, intentional communication, like the heartfelt note example, is pivotal. It's about building upon this foundation, actively learning, and applying effective communication strategies as an ongoing commitment. This isn't just about expressing love and appreciation but also about understanding your partner's needs and concerns. Open dialogue allows couples to navigate challenges, share aspirations, and align their goals, deepening their understanding of each other.

Moreover, when it comes to parenting, approaching it with the same level of intentional communication can create a harmonious family environment. As children grow, being attuned to their unique personalities and needs is crucial, and this requires constant communication between partners. It's about learning effective parenting techniques, sharing responsibilities, and adapting as a team. This approach can lay the groundwork for a supportive and nurturing family dynamic. Embracing continuous growth and learning in both marriage and parenting enables couples to fortify their connection and build a resilient foundation for a lifetime of shared joys and challenges.

When I take a moment to write Jessica a note that makes her feel seen and loved, it also gives me time to reflect and remind myself of my deep love for her. This simple action of writing a note not only makes her feel loved but also rekindles my own feelings of love.

Chapter III
Forging Unbreakable Bonds with Our Children

R aising a resilient, confident, and beloved child is no small feat. If you've picked up this book, you're at least up for the challenge.

Today, there's a battle our children face. Society heaps pressure on them, regardless of gender, nudging them to conceal their beliefs, morals, and values. As guardians, our fight isn't just about parenting; it's about supporting our kids in a world that often seems counterproductive.

Consider this: children are exposed to unsuitable content online at shockingly young ages. Social media platforms like TikTok, Snapchat, and Instagram bombard them with endless, sometimes meaningless, content. On average, kids are spending four to six hours a day on these apps.

Underage drinking is a widespread issue. Surveys like the National Survey on Drug Use and Health paint a concerning picture, with a significant percentage of young teens experimenting with alcohol. This is a wake-up call for all of us.

And consider marijuana. With its legal status changing in many states, it's easier than ever for young people to access it. What does this mean for our children's future?

We are our children's frontline of defense, guiding them through the war. We live in an era of sweeping technological change and proliferating patterns of youth substance use. Accordingly, we will explore tactics and knowledge to maneuver through such complexities. I will give down-to-earth counsel, share my experiences, and help you develop a viable system to make your ties with children everlasting. It is ultimately a journey toward creating a generation that can survive the challenges of today and stand as embodiments of honesty and compassion. It might be a fierce battle, but we have the weapons as well as the know-how to help our children stand firm in their faith and character.

LIFE IS A TEACHER: *WHERE TO FIND WISDOM, COURAGE, AND INSIGHT*

Remember the familiar phrase, "Do as I say, not as I do?" Our parents used this line often, but it's time to retire it if we're committed to being effective parents in our children's lives. There's just too much at stake. For our kids to develop a strong moral compass, character and integrity that is unshakable, and a desire to embrace faith, we must be willing to embody these qualities ourselves. Whenever we find ourselves feeling lost on our journey, we can always look to how Jesus lived and what He taught for guidance.

If we desire for our kids to live free from substance abuse, addiction, and low integrity, our commitment to walking the walk must be unwavering. Our kids are unlikely to seriously consider a life dedicated to morals, values, and Christ if we don't lead by example.

- If we don't want our children to be ensnared by drugs, we need to steer clear of drugs ourselves.
- To prevent them from falling into addiction, we must avoid those pitfalls too.

- For our children to develop a deep relationship with Christ, we should pray with them, teach them, and demonstrate what goodness looks like.
- If we aspire for our children to be strong leaders, we must lead by example and guide them.
- Teaching our children to respect others begins with how we show love, respect, and appreciation in our relationships, particularly toward their other parent.

The list goes on, but the essence is clear: the traits we wish to see in our children are deeply connected to our own behaviors and actions.

UNWAVERING LOYALTY: *BONDING WITH RESPECT, DEVOTION, AND CARE*

Growing up, I never had a stable father figure. My mom was married three times over my first eighteen years. Between each marriage, the men she dated would come and go, none sticking around for long. These men were often similar: heavy drinkers, abusive, and far from being good examples. Despite this, I don't hold any ill will about being raised in such an environment. I did for a long time, but now I view it as simply my experience, one that has shaped who I am today. We all have our own experiences, some easier, some harder. Our childhood experiences are just that—ours. They are what they are, and it's what we do with these experiences that shapes our future.

On the other hand, I was quite blessed with an amazing grandfather during my upbringing. He was my mom's dad and truly the best man I have ever known. My grandma and grandpa were married for fifty-two years before my grandpa passed away in 1998. They lived only three miles from us, so I saw them all the time.

As I reflect on my childhood with my grandpa, I realize how he stepped up and filled the father figure role. He never made a big deal about it or spoke of it openly. He just became an incredibly stable male role model in my life. Looking back, I believe he saw what was happening in my childhood and what I was missing. He knew I needed and yearned for a positive male role model, and he seamlessly stepped into that role.

He dedicated as much time to me as he could. My grandpa was always there to help with my homework and book reports. He showed me how to fix things, mow the lawn, and fish. He emphasized the importance of a man contributing at home too, doing tasks like cleaning, laundry, and cooking. He wasn't the only one doing these chores; my grandma pitched in as well, but he always did his part.

He was the one who picked me up from school for years, taking me to their house where I frequently had dinner. Once a month, I'd spend the weekend at their place. If I was there on a Saturday night, we'd wake up early Sunday for church. Sitting next to him, I'd sometimes hold his calloused, work-worn hands. He got those from his demanding job as a truck driver for 7Up, starting his day at 2:45 a.m. and leaving for work by 3:30 a.m. so he could make it home for dinner with his family. He was an insanely hard worker.

My grandpa was a deep man of faith. He would always listen intentionally to the pastor and the readings. At times I would look over and see his eyes closed as he listened to the Gospel and the homily. He really wanted to take in everything he could. My grandpa had terrible knees and was always in pain with osteoarthritis. He never complained about the pain, but you could see it when he walked or got up from his seat. However, he would still kneel in church during the segments when we were supposed to. I could tell he was in so much pain kneeling, but he still did it.

During prayers, he'd grip my hand tightly, a gesture that I found really cool as a kid. And leaving church, the pastor's face would always light up seeing my grandpa, who was genuinely loved by many for his authenticity, charisma, and interest in others.

After church, we'd drop into this quaint mom-and-pop donut shop for our Sunday treat. Then, off to my grandpa's house, where Grandma was just starting her day. There was something special about their kitchen table: Grandpa at the head, Grandma to his left. I always enjoyed sitting with them; the air was thick with their love for each other. Whenever Grandpa touched Grandma's hand, her eyes would lift, and a smile would bloom on her face. He'd often tell her she was beautiful or how much he loved her. And oh, the gratitude in her eyes— it was like watching a scene from an old romantic movie. You see, Grandpa's love was so tangible, so real, it filled the room. When he looked at her, his eyes sparkled with joy—it was like witnessing magic. This was a stark contrast to what I saw at home. My mom and stepdad's relationship was, well, it was a kind of storm—a tension so heavy it felt like a dark cloud hanging over our house.

But at Grandpa's, it was different. His love for Grandma was like a beacon of light, shining through that darkness. His words were more than just words; they were the language of his heart. He wasn't just going through the motions—every compliment, every "I love you" was heartfelt. He never let a day pass without expressing his love for her, not just once, but multiple times. It's something I never got tired of witnessing.

Growing up, my grandpa's house was my safe haven. This sense of security, I realize now, came from witnessing the intentional love between him and Grandma. Their bond seemed unbreakable, a testament to the power of love. That foundation of love not only made me feel safe but also brought a lot of happiness into my life.

These memories, looking back, were some of the most valuable lessons I've ever learned. I've taken these to heart, doubling down on them in my own life. Jessica and I have been together for twenty-seven years, married for twenty of those. A crucial part of being a dad and husband for me is passing these lessons on to our boys. They're getting a front-row seat to our relationship, and I'm all in on showing them what a great partnership looks like. It's not perfect—but it's pretty darn close.

Every single day, I make it a point to tell Jess how much I love her, to acknowledge her beauty, her kindness, her generous heart. And I don't hold back, especially in front of the boys. They've told me how much they appreciate seeing their parents in love. I believe it gives them a sense of safety and comfort. Our home has become a hub, not just for our boys but for their friends as well. The love Jess and I share so openly seems to have created this ripple effect.

THE LEADERSHIP SEED: *NURTURING INDEPENDENCE AS A FATHER*

Look into the heart of any dad, and you'll see something similar. We're all striving to raise kids who grow up to be strong, confident leaders, the kind who inspire others in the best ways. We dream of seeing our children thrive, believing in themselves, and living lives that are truly fulfilling. Our deepest wish is for them to lead with both confidence and certainty.

So, how exactly do we achieve this?

Well, I believe the key is to gently nudge them into slightly uncomfortable situations where they can be tested. It's in these moments they'll find their footing. When they succeed, their confidence skyrockets. And when they don't, they learn. Either way, they're growing, becoming more confident, and picking up invaluable life lessons along the way.

There's a verse in the Bible I often think about: "I can do all this through him who gives me strength" (Phil. 4:13). This verse echoes a powerful reminder we've had throughout the book: we're never alone. Even when we don't reach our goals, there are always lessons to be learned. Failure isn't the end; it's just a different kind of beginning, a chance to learn and grow. This is as true for young boys as it is for us grown men.

Back in 2019, I took a leap of faith. I led fifteen men, along with my boys Ethan (thirteen at the time), and Mason (eleven at the time) on a weekend retreat in the scenic mountains of Breckenridge, Colorado. It was a transformative experience. The weekend brimmed with activities—exercises and workshops aimed at elevating marriages, strengthening connections with their kids, and developing effective leadership skills. Ethan and Mason came along to soak in these lessons and witness everything firsthand.

The first day was a marathon of masterminding with my boys, Ethan and Mason. On the second day, we embarked on a remarkable journey to conquer Mt. Quandary, a majestic 14,165-foot peak, which turned out to be a twelve-hour round-trip hike to the top and back. The third day blended masterminding with the journey back home.

Bringing Ethan and Mason was crucial for two reasons. First, I wanted them to witness the power of genuine, iron-sharpens-iron friendships. The men at this retreat were extraordinary, embodying eagerness to learn, mutual respect, and a genuine care for each other's welfare. High-quality friendships like these are rare gems, and I hoped this experience would set a golden standard for the boys.

Secondly, this trip was a significant rite of passage for them. Ascending a fourteener is a formidable challenge, one that many don't dare to attempt. Yet, Ethan and Mason were ready and excited for the adventure. On the second day, we rose at 3:30 a.m., eager to meet the mountain. Unfortunately, Ethan woke up feeling unwell due to altitude sickness. He felt a bit dizzy, tired, and had a headache. Luckily, I hired a guide, who was also a skilled paramedic, and we thought it'd be best for Ethan to stay behind and recover. Mason, however, was in good spirits and set to make the climb. It was a tough decision, but definitely the right one.

We started on the trailhead around 4:30 a.m., with the intention of savoring the journey as much as the destination. Throughout the hike, I told Mason we would be stopping several times along the way to enjoy the views and to talk about new ways of living going from a young boy to a young man. I read him a letter I had written, outlining seven pillars of becoming a young man, a conversation we concluded at the summit's peak.

The trek up Mt. Quandary symbolized the final phase of Mason's childhood journey. Reaching the summit represented the climax and conclusion of his boyhood, while the descent signified his initial steps into young manhood. Remembering this excursion inspires me to share a story that encapsulates the essence of this transformative rite of passage.

If you've never climbed a fourteener like Mt. Quandary, it's an endeavor not to be underestimated. The hike is demanding and extensive. The thin air at 14,000 feet adds to the challenge, making breathing more laborious, even for the well-prepared. Mason and I embarked on this hike fully equipped, each with a CamelBak, snacks like dried fruits and nuts, beef jerky, electrolytes, Gatorade, rain gear, and extra clothing. I was carrying about twenty pounds, and Mason, considering his lighter frame, managed about ten pounds.

Mason, an athletic young man with a solid foundation in sports, was accustomed to physical exertion. His enthusiasm was apparent at the start, and he maintained a strong pace for the first few hours. However, around 10:30 a.m., six hours in, I could see he was beginning to tire. Leading the way, his steps showed slight unsteadiness as we climbed higher. When we were about ninety minutes from the summit, Mason's fatigue became more pronounced.

During one of our breaks, I mentioned to Mason that I noticed his tiredness and, thinking of safety, I suggested carrying his backpack full of supplies for him. However, Mason, being the kind of young man who never shies away from a challenge and doesn't like others carrying his burdens, flatly refused. He sees such help as a sign of weakness. Despite his initial refusal, I urged him again, prioritizing his safe ascent to the summit. He stood firm.

At this point, I had to assert my role as a father and play the "dad card," meaning I demanded that he take off his backpack so I could carry it for him. I told him it wasn't just a request anymore, but an order. He reluctantly took off his backpack and handed it to me. His head dropped slightly as I shouldered his bag along with mine. He seemed a bit defeated, maybe even a bit ashamed. I secured his backpack on top of mine and prepared to continue.

Now, carrying both my and Mason's packs, I was determined to ensure his comfort over mine. Mason resumed leading us up the mountain, his head still lowered, moving at a slower pace, his body language reflecting shame and defeat. Catching up to him, I walked side by side with him and tried to offer some fatherly encouragement.

I said to him, "Mason, I see you're upset about giving up your bag. I get it. I'm sure you feel like it's a sign of weakness to ask for help, but it's really not. It's about being safe. Who knows, maybe later in this hike, I'll be the one needing your help!"

He responded saying: "I know, Dad. I just didn't want the help. I wanted to do it all on my own."

"I know, son, but at times, every man needs some help. Again, maybe before this hike is done, you will be helping me."

Looking back, I realize my words to Mason might have sounded condescending. At the time, I didn't think I'd need help from my eleven-year-old son. After all, I had experience with fourteeners and prided myself on my physical fitness. But I underestimated the unexpected lessons and humility I would gain from Mason on our descent.

We summited Mt. Quandary just past noon, after a nearly eight-hour climb. Out of the twelve men we started with, only seven, including us, reached the top. Four men turned back at the halfway mark, and one couldn't leave the Airbnb due to altitude sickness.

Reaching the summit, we had lunch, took stunning photos, and I finished reading the letter to Mason. It was an emotional moment; Mason's tears flowed as he heard the letter, and seeing him cry made me cry too. He expressed how much the letter and the experience meant to him, something he'd cherish for life.

As we started our descent, about ten minutes in with several hours ahead, my quads cramped up intensely. The pain shot down my legs and into my lower back. Initially, I tried to ignore it, hoping it would fade as I moved. But it only worsened, and I had to stop. I explained to Mason that my legs were cramping, so I took off the backpacks and my Camel-Bak, and I stretched my legs. After a ten-minute break and drinking plenty of water, I felt ready to continue the descent.

Just twenty minutes into the descent, my legs locked up again, this time even more severely. I stopped immediately, taking everything off my back and started stretching on the ground. The cramps were intense, and no amount of aggressive stretching seemed to help. Mason looked on, visibly worried; he had never seen me this vulnerable. The pain in my quads was excruciating, and I was at a loss about how to get down the mountain.

Thoughts of being airlifted off the mountain began to cross my mind, a disappointing end to what had been an incredible journey with Mason. Our guide advised that I needed electrolytes urgently. I began drinking Gatorade and eating beef jerky and bananas, hoping to alleviate the cramps.

After roughly thirty minutes of stretching, hydrating, and refueling, the cramps finally eased. I felt a sense of relief, believing that the worst was over. I stood up, reached for my CamelBak, and started to look for our backpacks. To my surprise, I couldn't find them anywhere. Then I saw Mason, wearing his CamelBak and both our backpacks. I was astounded. My son, who weighed only eighty pounds, was carrying an extra twenty pounds on his back. I approached him, insisting that he give me the backpacks, but he refused. Even after I demanded again, he stood his ground.

What unfolded next is something I'll always remember. Mason met my eyes and said, "You told me there might come a time on this hike where you needed my help, just like I needed yours. You said being a man means being brave enough to ask for and accept help when it's most needed. I want to help you now." With tears in my eyes and every instinct wanting to say no, I simply embraced him. This was his moment of stepping up, and I couldn't take that away from him.

I decided to let him carry my backpack for as long as he felt able to, ensuring it was safe. For the next two hours as we made our way down, Mason led us, bravely shouldering over thirty pounds on his back. I had always imagined the precious memories we'd create on this mountain, but this particular moment was beyond anything I had anticipated. My pride in him was immense. His gesture of helping me in my vulnerable state became a pivotal part of his passage into manhood. Throughout that twelve-hour journey, Mason went from being a little boy to emerging as a young man. The entire experience—the climb, the conversations, the scenery, and especially the descent—will remain one of our most treasured memories.

Over the years, I've pushed Mason to achieve things that seemed beyond his reach. When he was ten, he became a bestselling author with his book *Never Give Up No Matter What*, inspired by his time as a little league football player. The book, a story about persistence despite limited playing time, has sold over ten thousand copies. His success at such a young age is extraordinary. Furthermore, Mason has shared his story at several personal development seminars, overcoming his discomfort with public speaking to inspire others. His resilience and willingness to challenge himself are truly inspiring.

At the dinner table, we encourage the boys to lead us in prayer, a task that can be quite intimidating for young men. Ethan, my oldest, at seventeen, took the bold step of starting his own car wash and detailing business. He faced his fears of failure and the unfamiliarity head-on. There were some speed bumps along the way, but that's beneficial. Gaining early life lessons is invaluable compared to having no experience at all.

When confronted with challenges, we ask our boys to consider how they might pray for guidance. It's easy to feel alone when facing difficulties, but praying for guidance helps to relieve that feeling of isolation, reminding them of our God's constant presence.

In social scenarios, especially around their peers, we constantly remind and encourage them to follow their moral compass. It's a given that within any group, there's likely to be pressure to engage in wrong or morally questionable activities. There are always those who are reluctant to follow the crowd but are too afraid to speak up. We remind our boys that their voice could be the one that others are silently hoping will stand against peer pressure.

Putting our boys in leadership roles helps to build their confidence, preparing them to lead even when we're not around. Constant reinforcement to lead through their faith and moral compass increases the chances that they'll make better decisions, impacting not only their lives but also those of their peers.

Raising young men to be confident leaders who follow a faith-based moral compass isn't always straightforward. As parents, it's our role to continuously guide and be their advocates. This kind of leadership doesn't ensure a life free from problems or resistance. I always remind my boys that their way of leading might make sense to some but not to others, similar to how Jesus faced challenges and persecution. But that's okay. It's all part of being a faith leader and a beloved son of God.

RESPECTFUL LOVING: *SETTING AN EXAMPLE OF TRUE AFFECTION*

Countless times, parenting experts on podcasts have discussed a key topic regarding raising children. The question usually goes something like this: How can we bring up strong, confident, and independent young individuals who won't tolerate being mistreated by anyone?

The simplest answer is to lead by example and demonstrate profound love and respect within the family. Children are observant and take note of how their parents interact with each other. As they grow, they are learning about respect, love, and how to communicate effectively. Whether it's through small acts like opening doors, sharing household responsibilities, or the manner of speaking to each other, children absorb these moments. By treating each other with respect and love, we set a standard for how they should expect to be treated in their own relationships. The principle of loving others as one would want to be loved is a cornerstone in this learning process.

Ephesians 5:25–30: Husbands, love your wives, just as Christ loved the church and gave himself up for her to make her holy, cleansing her by the washing with water through the word, and to present her to himself as a radiant church, without stain or wrinkle or any other blemish, but holy and blameless. In this same way, husbands ought to love their wives as their own bodies. He who loves his wife loves himself. After all, no one ever hated their own body, but they feed and care for their body, just as Christ does the church—for we are members of his body. "For this reason, a man will leave his father and mother and be united to his wife, and the two will become one flesh."

Navigating the complexities of relationships can be challenging. Relationships go through phases of closeness and distance, and children are, as just mentioned, always observing and learning, regardless of the phase. Even the most resilient relationships face challenges, but these periods are often temporary and can affect children less. Relationships that are built on a foundation of mutual respect and understanding tend to navigate these challenges more successfully. When experiencing difficult times, it might be indicative of a need to focus more on nurturing the relationship and maintaining open communication.

Here are some ways to demonstrate to our children, irrespective of gender, what a good person looks like and how they express love:

Open and Respectful Communication

It's essential to keep our voices calm, avoid name-calling, and listen with genuine curiosity and appreciation. Learning and demonstrating conflict resolution skills sets a positive example for all children.

Never Underestimate the Power of Manners

Consistently using polite expressions like "Please," "Thank you," and "Excuse me" has a significant impact. Children, observing these manners, learn the importance of courtesy.

Physical Affection without an Agenda

Simple acts of affection—holding hands, a hug, a kiss on the forehead, guiding with a hand on the back, pulling out chairs, opening doors are all powerful demonstrations of care. These gestures, though small, are impactful, and children are observant of them.

Praying Together as a Family

Engaging in prayer with our partner in front of our children, including them in the process, is meaningful. It shows the value of something greater than ourselves, reinforcing a foundation of love and honor in relationships. Additionally, praying together enhances family intimacy and closeness.

Communicate, Communicate, Communicate

Moving beyond mere management of household tasks, engaging in deeper conversations is crucial. Discussing dreams, goals, emotions, daily ups and downs, and asking for advice in front of children shows them what healthy communication looks like.

By loving our partners openly and strongly in front of our children, we teach them what exceptional relationships look like. This way, they grow up understanding and expecting love and respect in all their relationships, and will be less likely to settle for anything less than what they've witnessed at home.

THE ART OF HEARTFELT LISTENING: *DEEPENING BONDS THROUGH UNDERSTANDING*

In the perpetual dance between dads and their children, one powerful act takes center stage: listening.

This simple action is about much more than merely hearing words. It's about cementing an even stronger bond and offering a haven that will last for life. Imagine a child's words as the vibrant hues on a painter's palette, each one revealing a facet of their unique identity. When fathers actively listen, they reveal the canvas for a portrait built on understanding and trust.

As kids navigate the maze of growing up, having a dad who listens becomes their guiding compass. It's like having a trusted companion who understands the twists and turns of life's journey. When fathers truly listen, they get a backstage pass to their children's thoughts, fears, and dreams. Amidst the rollercoaster ride of adolescence, where figuring out who you are can feel like solving a puzzle, a dad's listening ear becomes a steady anchor, offering comfort, guidance, and a constant reminder of their worth.

I vividly recall a short YouTube reel titled "It's Not About the Nail." Picture this: a married couple sits on their couch, their faces partially obscured. The woman is venting to her husband about a headache that has taken over her day. She goes into detail, describing the excruciating pain and its impact on her work, quality of life, and even her sleep. The camera pans to the man's face, revealing a look of confusion and mounting frustration.

As the camera finally reveals the full view of the woman's face, the source of their distress becomes clear: a nail protrudes prominently from her forehead. The woman is in visible distress, and the nail's presence seems undeniable. The man patiently listens before finally stating the obvious: "Well, you do have a nail sticking straight out of your head."

The woman replies, even more frustrated, "It's not about the nail!"

"Are you sure? Because I bet if we just pull that thing out, everything will be fine!"

"You always do this! You always try to fix it when all I need you to do is listen!" she replies.

The man, now extremely annoyed, agrees to listen as she continues her emotional release. She goes on for a few more minutes, expressing her concern over disrupted sleep, snagged clothes, and hindered work performance.

When she finishes, the man looks at her with compassion and says, "That sounds really hard." In that moment of empathy and understanding, you see her visibly soften. She feels seen, heard, and safe—not only essential needs for a child from a parent but also fundamental pillars for any relationship.

As fathers, we are naturally inclined to fix problems and find solutions. This inherent trait, while admirable, can also be a double-edged sword in relationships. When we perceive an opportunity to solve a problem or alleviate pain, we often jump at the chance. Our motivation stems from our deep love and desire to protect our children from any form of discomfort or distress. When the answer seems painfully obvious, we instinctively want to swoop in, offer solutions, and direct traffic, so to speak.

However, this "fixer" approach often backfires, sending unintended messages that contradict our true intentions. We might argue that our attentiveness allows us to provide clear solutions, but this often isn't how our children perceive it. When we start offering solutions, it can come across as if we've stopped listening and are solely focused on our suggestions. As a result, they feel unheard and frustrated, which is the opposite of our desired outcome.

Moreover, this approach can convey a lack of trust in their ability to navigate challenges on their own. It can feel condescending as if we're suggesting solutions they've already considered. Again, it sends an unintended message of "I don't believe you can figure this out, so let me tell you how to solve it." It's safe to say that these are not the messages we want to convey as dads.

When our children seek to vent, they yearn to be seen, heard, safe, and connected. They crave empathy and validation. We can be more effective listeners by simply acknowledging their emotions—anger, frustration, sadness, overwhelmed, or any other relevant feeling. It may seem simple, but it's often all that's needed. Of course, there are instances when our children genuinely seek our help in resolving dilemmas. However, in most cases, all they need is our validation and a listening ear.

PILLARS OF SUPPORT: *BEING THERE IN TIMES OF NEED*

There's a simple four-step process you can follow when your children are going through a difficult time, experiencing intense emotions, and seeking your support. We've taught this process to thousands of fathers over the years, and it has worked wonders for communication, connection, and the overall relationship.

Before we delve into the process, let's briefly discuss "intense emotions" and what they mean. First and foremost, emotions are neither good nor bad; they simply exist. Sadness, anger, and so on are not "bad emotions." Emotions are an integral part of the human experience. However, our interpretation of emotions can lead to labeling them as "bad" or "weak" or "negative."

For instance, if we experience sadness, some of us may perceive ourselves as weak. Similarly, if we feel anger, we may feel guilty for experiencing that emotion. Again, sadness and anger are not inherently good or bad; they are simply part of our human experience. In our household, all emotions are welcome. However, not all behaviors are. If you feel anger at home, that's okay. But if you express that anger by throwing a chair through the window, that's a different story.

It's crucial to understand that when our children experience what they perceive as a negative emotion, they likely already feel some degree of shame or guilt for even having that emotion. Sometimes, we can exacerbate that feeling of shame or guilt by our reactions.

For example, if our child comes home and tells us why they're so angry at their best friend for saying something hurtful, we tend to try to lessen the burden of that emotion by saying something like, "That doesn't sound that bad. I know this seems like a big deal because you're only thirteen, but in the grand scheme of things, it's not a big deal. Why are you so upset?"

Reading these words back to ourselves may make us sound insensitive. However, if you ask most of us caregivers, we're genuinely curious and want to understand why they're so upset. We're not trying to belittle them or their feelings. When we say things like "that doesn't sound that bad," what we're really trying to do is help them gain some perspective and alleviate some of the pain and pressure they feel.

This response might seem like a good idea in the moment because we think we're de-escalating our child's anger. However, in reality, we're compounding it. Again, this is not our intention. Our intention as fathers stems from a deep desire to protect our child's feelings.

Jesus was an incredible empathetic listener. He often took the time to listen to people's questions, doubts, and needs. He engaged in meaningful conversations with individuals, addressing their concerns and providing guidance (e.g., the Samaritan woman at the well in John 4:1–42).

So, how can we be more effective listeners and caregivers?

We can follow a simple yet effective four-step process. This process fosters a strong connection between dad and child. When our children are expressing an "intense" emotion (sadness, anger, overwhelm, etc.), we can:

1. Globalize
2. Normalize
3. Invite more
4. Ask how to best support them

Globalizing involves labeling the emotion but placing the spotlight and attention on the situation rather than the person. When our children (or even people in general) experience intense emotions, we can help ease the guilt or shame by focusing on why the situation is frustrating, infuriating, annoying, overwhelming, or sad, emphasizing the situation rather than the person. For example, if they're angry about their best friend saying something hurtful, we can respond with "The fact that they said that to you sounds infuriating" versus "Sounds like YOU are furious." When we shift the focus from the person to the situation, it's incredibly disarming and puts them at ease. It makes them feel seen, heard, and safe.

The second step is to *normalize*. When our children (and people in general) feel a heavy emotion, they typically feel alone. They forget that anyone in their situation would probably feel the same way. When we feel alone with our intense emotions, we can experience an even greater sense of guilt and isolation. So, when we normalize, we take away that loneliness, isolation, and heaviness. For example, using the same situation above, after we globalize with "the fact that they said that to you sounds infuriating" (globalize), we can follow with "Who wouldn't be infuriated if their best friend said that?" (normalize). When we normalize and globalize, we provide another layer of validation, empathy, and connection.

The third step in this process is to *invite more.* Inviting for more involves saying, "Tell me more about that." I'm a strong advocate for removing the word "why" from my vocabulary. The word "why" psychologically puts the other person on the defensive. It feels accusatory and intrusive as if they've done something wrong. It can be as simple as asking, "Why did they say that to you?" Suddenly, they are on the defensive, and the connection we're trying to establish becomes more complicated. Instead, saying "Tell me more" is incredibly effective in helping us understand why something happened or why they feel the way they do. They will feel invited to share more instead of feeling psychologically cornered.

The final step is to *ask how to best support them* by asking, "How can I best support you right now? What feels right to you?" We ask this final question because they will most likely tell you the most effective thing to do next. They might reply with, "Nothing, I just needed to talk about it." They might also say, "I don't know what to do about it. Can you help me figure it out?" The most important thing is that you ask. Even if they have no clue what to tell you what is best, they will appreciate the question because they know you care.

So, let's put it all together. When a situation like this arises, follow these four steps:

1. Globalize: "The fact that they said that sounds infuriating."
2. Normalize: "Who wouldn't be furious? Anyone would be really upset."
3. Invite more: "Tell me more about it."
4. Ask how to best support them: "How can I best support you right now? What feels right to you?"

WHEN INNER BEAUTY BLOSSOMS: *COMPASSIONATE CONFIDENCE AND LIMITLESS SELF-WORTH*

In the digital age, where screens have become windows to a world that often feels like a never-ending highlight reel, parents face a unique and unprecedented challenge in helping their children navigate the comparison trap. As today's parents, we are pioneers in the complex terrain of parenting our children through the age of social media. We are the first generation tasked with helping our young ones navigate the potentially harmful waters of Instagram, TikTok,

Snapchat, and more, where the quest for likes and the allure of filters can subtly erode their confidence, self-esteem, and mental well-being. It's a challenge we may be, at times, blissfully unaware of, but the impact is profound. As fathers, we stand at the forefront of this battle to safeguard our children's sense of self in a world where comparison is constant, and the line between reality and the curated online persona blurs.

Let's discuss some pertinent research. The impact of social media on self-esteem and body image is particularly concerning for young people. Numerous studies have shown a link between social media usage and body dissatisfaction among adolescents. Constant exposure to idealized and often unrealistic beauty standards on platforms like Instagram and TikTok can lead to lower self-esteem and negative body image.[1] A report by the UK's Royal Society for Public Health found that Instagram had the most negative impact on young people's mental health, particularly regarding body image and self-esteem.[2]

---

1. Jasmine Fardouly et al., "Social Comparisons on Social Media: The Impact of Facebook on Young Women's Body Image Concerns and Mood," *Body Image* 13 (March 2015): 38–45. doi:10.1016/j.bodyim.2014.12.002.

2. Royal Society for Public Health, "Status of Mind: Social Media and Young People's Mental Health and Wellbeing," May 2017, https://www.rsph .org.uk/static/uploaded/d125b27c-0b62-41c5-a2c0155a8887cd01.pdf.

The increased use of social media has been associated with higher levels of anxiety, depression, and loneliness in young people. Cyberbullying and online harassment can further exacerbate these issues.[3] A study published in JAMA Pediatrics in 2019 found that the use of social media is linked to an increase in the risk of major depressive disorder among adolescent girls.[4] While these statistics may also apply to young boys, research has shown that the negative impact is generally more pronounced for young girls.

Social media platforms often encourage constant comparison, whether with peers, celebrities, or influencers, which can lead to feelings of inadequacy and increased stress.[5] Research has shown that kids who spend more time on social media are more likely to engage in appearance-related comparisons and experience negative emotional consequences as a result.[6]

---

3. Brian A. Primack et al., "Social Media Use and Perceived Social Isolation Among Young Adults in the U.S.," *American Journal of Preventative Medicine* 53, no. 1 (2017): 1–8.

4. M. Shychuk, N. Joseph, L. A. Thompson, "Social Media Use in Children and Adolescents," *JAMA Pediatrics* 176, no. 7 (May 2022): 730, doi:10.1001/jamapediatrics.2022.1134.

5. Marika Tiggemann and Amy Slater, "NetGirls: The Internet, Facebook, and Body Image Concern in Adolescent Girls," *International Journal of Eating Disorders* 46, no. 6 (2013): 630–33.

6. American Psychological Association, "Health Advisory on Social Media Use in Adolescence," May 2023, https://www.apa.org/topics/social-media-internet/health-advisory-adolescent-social-media-use.pdf.

Let's be honest with ourselves. We are the first generation of parents leading the charge in this battle. For most of us, it feels like a barren field with hidden landmines everywhere. We are unsure of how to navigate this complex terrain and protect our children's hearts and minds. However, the fight is real, and so are the potential pitfalls. Experts increasingly warn that we may not fully comprehend the devastating impact on this generation of kids until they are adults. This mirrors the situation with smoking, where the health implications were not fully understood until years later when people started dying from cancer and other smoking-related diseases. The same could be true for the effects of social media.

So, what is a parent to do? Many of us are looking for new ways to fight this battle, searching for a new hack or strategy. However, the answer may lie not in something new but in revisiting the fundamental principles that truly matter, such as our Christian values. Consider this: genuine beauty sprouts from the heart, spreading outward into limitless worth. Our inner beauty blossoms when we cultivate our kindness, compassion, and empathy; this resembles a flower unfolding its petals. Accordingly, we cannot doubt ourselves and allow others to validate our existence. We must realize that our children's values should not be determined by fleeting "likes" but found instead within the depths of our hearts.

LEADING WITH LIGHT: *SETTING AN EXAMPLE IN YOUR RELATIONSHIPS*

I understand that this is a recurring theme throughout the book, but it's crucial to address its significance in fostering confidence and self-respect in our children. Remember, the most impactful life lessons are caught, not taught. If we want our children to possess self-respect, self-love, and confidence, we must embody those qualities ourselves. It's essential for our children to witness us treating our minds, bodies, and spirits with respect. We must be committed to modeling these behaviors in our own lives.

Practice Self-Compassion

Many of us are unduly harsh on ourselves. We not only have the ability to berate ourselves internally, but we can also be incredibly cruel to ourselves through our external voice. Our children may overhear us criticizing our age, physical appearance, intelligence, or financial situation. God desires for us to love ourselves. The fascinating aspect of compassion is that most of us extend more compassion to our best friends, children, partners, and even coworkers than we do to ourselves. How would our internal and external dialogue change if we were a bit more kind to ourselves? What would it look like if we applied the same standards of self-talk to ourselves as we do to our children? If we want our children to cultivate lifelong self-love, we need to adopt that same approach for ourselves.

Embrace Imperfections

Imperfections are what make us human and unique. There is no perfect human being on this planet. We all have flaws, and they are what define us. Here's a funny and true story: My fifteen-year-old son enjoys teasing me about my skinny legs. I'm 6'1" and weigh around 175 pounds. I've been working out regularly for the past thirty years, including dedicated leg training, but my legs stubbornly refuse to bulk up. My upper body is noticeably more muscular than my lower body. I used to despise it, but now I just laugh it off and embrace it. I have two perfectly functional legs that enable me to walk, run, and engage in sports with my children. When my children make fun of my legs, I simply laugh along and say, "Yep, these are mine. They help me live my best life with you guys. I wouldn't trade them for anything." When we truly reflect on it, our imperfections are what make us relatable to others. Perfection is unattainable and unrelatable. God loves us for who we are, flaws and all. So, why shouldn't we love ourselves the same way? Why can't our children love themselves the same way?

Encourage Self-Respect

Instill in your child the importance of valuing themselves as a child of God. Help them understand that their worth is not determined by their appearance but by their identity in Christ. Encourage them to love and respect themselves. When we compare ourselves to others, we set ourselves up for failure. Comparison is a thief of joy. Instead of seeking validation for our self-love, self-respect, and confidence from social media, peers, and media-defined beauty standards, we can recognize that they are a beloved child of God. God is love and grace. The media can be a deceptive trap when it comes to self-love.

Teach Service to Others

One way to reduce our self-focus is to redirect our attention toward others. The Bible is brimming with passages emphasizing the importance of serving others. If we examine the roots of anxiety, low self-esteem, and low self-respect, we discover that they arise from excessive introspection. The world as we perceive it becomes solely about ourselves and our shortcomings. However, when we recognize that the world extends beyond ourselves and embrace service to others, our perspective shifts dramatically. When we contribute, bring joy to others, and foster peace, it profoundly impacts our self-perception.

A few simple verses on this are: "Do nothing out of selfish ambition or vain conceit. Rather, in humility value others above yourselves, not looking to your own interests but each of you to the interests of the others" (Phil. 2:3–4). The Apostle Paul encourages people to prioritize the needs and interests of others over their own, promoting a selfless attitude.

The apostle Paul states: "Each of you should use whatever gift you have received to serve others, as faithful stewards of God's grace in its various forms"

(1 Peter 4:10). This verse emphasizes that God has given each person unique gifts and abilities, and we should use them to serve others as stewards of God's grace.

In Acts 20:35, Paul declares, "In everything I did, I showed you that by this kind of hard work we must help the weak, remembering the words the Lord Jesus himself said: 'It is more blessed to give than to receive.'" Here, Paul quotes Jesus, emphasizing the idea that giving and serving others bring blessings and fulfillment.

The Bible consistently teaches that serving others is not only a divine mandate but also a source of blessing and spiritual growth. When we serve others with a compassionate spirit, we are aligning with our higher purpose and embodying the principles of service. Additionally, we often find joy, contentment, and a deeper sense of purpose in serving individuals who require our assistance.

GROWING TOGETHER: *CULTIVATING SUSTAINABLE CONNECTIONS*

We all aspire to have the ideal marriage or relationship with our partner—to realize the dream of unparalleled intimacy, consistently clear and meaningful communication, and the ability to resolve conflicts quickly and effectively, without losing patience or tempers. When it comes to our children, our desires are no less ambitious. We strive for an unbreakable bond, unlimited patience, and to be more than just a parent—to be our kids' hero. However, the reality of relationships is that they are dynamic, complex, and continuously evolving. They can also feel stuck or stagnant at times. Measuring progress in relationships is often challenging due to their fluid and ever-changing nature.

In the midst of these complex relationship dynamics, it's essential to focus on enjoying the journey rather than obsessing over achieving perfection. Striving for an idealized version of a relationship often leads to frustration and disappointment. Relationships naturally ebb and flow like a river; they have their calm moments and their turbulent ones. Progress in relationships is not about achieving a state of flawlessness but is more about a shared commitment to growth and improvement. It's about facing challenges together, fostering open communication, being vulnerable, and practicing empathy.

These actions pave the way for genuine connections that can shape us in amazing ways.

In the intricate dance of relationships, it's important to release the expectation of constant perfection and appreciate the beauty in imperfection. Again, the bumps and detours we encounter are not setbacks but opportunities to learn, grow, and adapt. Progress lies in the small, deliberate actions we take daily—actively listening, showing gratitude, and striving to understand each other better. It demands a commitment to personal growth, as individuals and relationships continuously evolve. By focusing on this kind of progress, fathers can lay a resilient foundation for their relationships, creating a journey that strengthens love, understanding, and connection within the complex dynamics of family life.

While there are aspects of our lives where progress is more "black and white," such as in fitness or finance, relationships operate on a spectrum that's less quantifiable. Fitness progress can be tracked through various metrics like weight, body fat, BMI, physical performance, and bloodwork results. Financial health can be assessed through budgeting, net worth, debt reduction, and savings.

Relationships, however, are subject to more fluid and dynamic measures.

Relationships are nuanced and fluid by nature. While we can mark milestones like anniversaries or cherish shared memories, the true essence of a relationship transcends any quantifiable measurements. They thrive in the intangible—the moments of understanding, shared laughter, and unwavering support. Unlike the straightforward feedback of a financial statement or a fitness tracker, the progress in relationships is often more deeply felt than explicitly calculated. Furthermore, the dynamics of relationships go beyond individual achievements.

Unlike personal fitness goals or financial targets, the health of a relationship is founded on the synergy and collaborative effort between individuals. It's about a combined journey, transcending numerical measurements. The success of a relationship is measured not in individual metrics but in shared experiences, effective communication, and mutual growth. While fitness and finance are important aspects of personal progress, relationships bloom in the realms of emotion, empathy, and connection. Recognizing and valuing the unique nature of relationship progress allows us to navigate its complexities with a deeper appreciation for the qualitative elements that make it truly significant.

Some days, the connection within our relationships can feel heavy, strained, and distant. Other days, it feels connected, intimate, and secure. What truly matters is consistently doing the right things to deepen that connection. To have more meaningful conversations with our partners that are both connecting and fulfilling, we must engage in such dialogues proactively. Just as we create and execute a fitness plan to elevate our physical health, we must approach our relationships with the same level of intention and consistency.

Building and maintaining a deep connection within relationships is an ongoing process, demanding intentional effort. Like the ebb and flow of a river, emotional dynamics in a partnership vary. Recognizing that not every day will feel seamlessly connected allows us to move through challenges with resilience and understanding. Similar to how a fitness regimen requires consistent effort to see results, relationships thrive under sustained investment. This means not only celebrating the good times but also navigating the tough times together, with a commitment to continually deepening the connection. Moreover, the quality of our connection in relationships often mirrors the habits and rituals we cultivate. Engaging in shared activities, showing appreciation, and actively listening are key to weaving a strong bond. Creating a positive cycle of intentional actions further strengthens this bond. As we aim for consistent, fulfilling connections, being mindful of our actions and their impact on the relationship becomes vital. Like a well-crafted fitness plan, building a profound connection requires dedication and adaptability, adjusting to the changing nature of relationships.

Many of us, however, are not creating tactical habits to connect with our partners or children. We might resort to default questions like "How was your day?" that don't typically foster a deeper relationship. What's important is doing the most effective things that deepen our connections at home. Saying "Tell me about the best part of your day" encourages your partner or child to reflect on the positive aspects of their day, creating an emotional response and a deeper connection. This is more effective than the standard, "How was your day?" which often elicits brief and unengaging answers.

Taking your partner on a date night with intimate conversation starters can also ignite a deeper connection. Asking questions like "What is something I do that makes you feel most loved?" or "Think of a time in our relationship when you felt incredibly connected to me. What were we doing and why did you pick that moment?" fosters meaningful dialogue. This is more effective than discussing high-level managerial aspects of family life, which, while necessary, don't create as profound a connection.

Discussing faith and praying together as a family can significantly strengthen your bond. Questions like "When did you feel God's presence in your life today?" or "How did you lean into your faith today when you needed it most?" help deepen your family's spiritual connection. This is more impactful than just attending church weekly without engaging in deeper discussions about faith.

In focusing on progress with our relationships, it's about being tactical with the emotional connection. Leading with connection and conversational excellence starts with generative questions that delve deeper into our feelings and experiences, fostering a stronger bond in our most cherished relationships.

Chapter IV

Illuminating Purposeful Paths

My mom's journey to higher education was an extraordinary one. She didn't embark on her college studies until her late thirties, having spent much of my childhood navigating various jobs and career paths. Her unwavering determination to make ends meet, despite the challenges, left an indelible mark on me.

Throughout my childhood, she emphasized the importance of education, often reiterating that not pursuing a college degree had resulted in missed opportunities for well-paying jobs and a fulfilling career. When she finally decided to pursue her education in the late 1980s, she juggled her studies with her demanding real estate agent job, working evenings, weekends, and whenever possible to fit in coursework.

As a teenager, our lives were like ships passing in the night. Between the ages of nine and fourteen, I barely saw her due to her hectic schedule. I could sense her regret at having to lead life that way, but she never wavered in her pursuit of a better future for herself and our family.

The constant message I received from her was clear: "Focus on your studies, get good grades, and aim for a prestigious college. A good education will open doors to high-paying jobs and a fulfilling career. Become a doctor, lawyer, or something that pays well, and you'll find happiness and fulfillment."

Over the years, working with countless individuals, I've realized that this message resonated with many fathers of our generation. The belief that educational excellence, followed by a high-paying career, was the key to happiness was deeply ingrained. While this formula may have worked for some, it certainly wasn't a guarantee of happiness for all. Many individuals followed this path, only to find themselves unfulfilled despite their professional success. Of course, I'm not against pursuing financial success; I believe that when used wisely, money can be a powerful tool to amplify our impact, enhance our lives, and provide for our families. Money can open doors to generosity and create a safety net during unforeseen circumstances. However, financial wealth is not the sole determinant of happiness. I've encountered individuals who have amassed immense wealth yet remain deeply unhappy and unfulfilled. Conversely, I've met millionaires who find immense joy in their work, their lives invigorated by their passions. And I've seen individuals with modest incomes radiate contentment and fulfillment.

The bottom line is this: happiness is not simply a product of financial success.

Growing up under the constant message of "Education, good grades, prestigious college, high-paying job, doctor or lawyer equals happiness," I diligently followed that path. I excelled in high school, attending an all-boys Catholic college preparatory institution. Considering the tuition of $4,000 per year in the early 1990s, I secured a work grant to cover the expenses.

Throughout my four years of high school, I worked on campus every Saturday, starting at 10 a.m. I took on various tasks as needed, from assisting in the Jesuit priests' kitchen to landscaping and general upkeep. It was simple manual labor, but

I didn't mind. It allowed me to attend school tuition-free and instilled in me a strong work ethic. It also provided opportunities to connect with my teachers, the Jesuit priests who resided on campus.

Most of my high school classmates came from affluent families and never experienced financial hardship. In retrospect, the opportunity to work for my education was invaluable. It fostered a deeper appreciation for everything I had. Additionally, I noticed that the Jesuits I worked for respected me, recognizing that my background differed from that of my peers.

I successfully gained admission to a reputable college, pursuing a degree in health management with a minor in nutrition. My passion for health, exercise science, sports medicine, and nutrition drove my choice of study. Healthy living and exercise have been central to my life since childhood. I eagerly attended my college classes, fascinated by the knowledge they imparted. I couldn't wait to apply this knowledge in my future career.

When I informed my mom about my chosen degree, she expressed significant concern. She assumed that a four-year bachelor's degree in science would only qualify me to become a personal trainer.

While her assumption wasn't entirely inaccurate, the degree opened doors to various career paths in corporate wellness, working with professional sports teams, or even pursuing a master's degree in physical therapy. However, she consistently warned me against pursuing such a niche field, fearing that if I failed to find a job in my area of study, my employment prospects would be limited. She cautioned me about the potential for low pay and the likelihood of long-term unhappiness and financial struggles.

Despite my resistance to her message, her concerns held some validity. Finding a decent-paying job in my chosen field proved challenging. The average starting salary for someone in corporate wellness ranged from $28,000 to $32,000 per year. This realization struck me during my senior year, just before graduation.

To be honest, I panicked. Not only had I self-funded my high school education, but I was also facing a significant student loan burden. By graduation, I owed around $40,000. The realization that owning a home and a car, and providing for a family might require working two jobs was disheartening. I questioned my decision to follow my passion and purpose, fearing that financial stability might forever elude me. Perhaps I should have listened to my mom and opted for a more secure career path, such as medicine, law, or business. After all, didn't a good job equate to good pay and, consequently, a good life?

Upon realizing this, I quickly began exploring new fields and industries that offered higher salaries, even if it meant sacrificing my initial career aspirations. At the time, I was working as a personal trainer to support myself and pay for college. One of my clients, a pharmaceutical sales representative, exuded an infectious positivity and enthusiasm for her work. During a training session, I confided in her about my dilemma, and she passionately described the rewards and fulfillment she found in her sales career. In the mid-1990s, she earned a base salary of $65,000, along with bonuses, a company car, an expense account, and various perks. Her total compensation easily surpassed six figures, a substantial amount in that era.

Intrigued by the financial potential and the promise of a satisfying career, I wholeheartedly pursued the pharmaceutical industry. I was determined to secure a position, regardless of whether I would truly enjoy the work. The money and perks, I believed, would bring me the happiness I sought.

Having grown up in poverty, I experienced severe financial hardship throughout my college years. I often struggled to afford groceries and make my meager rent of $245 per month. There were instances when I filled my car's fuel tank with just $3, hoping it would be enough to get me to and from work until my next paycheck.

Living in such constant financial straits was an intolerable reality. I was determined to break the cycle of poverty and financial struggle that had plagued my family for generations. I couldn't bear the thought of subjecting my future family to the same hardships I had endured.

A few months after graduating, I landed my first job at Bristol Myers Squibb after interviewing with several pharmaceutical companies. My starting salary was $45,000, with a car allowance, bonuses, and various perks. In total, my annual compensation amounted to approximately $70,000, double what I had projected to earn in my initial field of study. Additionally, the role remained within the healthcare sector, aligning with my passion for health and wellness. This new position served as the launching pad for a successful twenty-two-year career in the pharmaceutical and surgical device industries.

Over the course of those twenty-two years, I steadily ascended the corporate ladder, progressing from sales representative to trainer, regional specialist, regional manager, and ultimately reaching the executive level as national sales director. From 2010 to 2021, my average annual compensation, including bonuses, car allowance, travel expenses, and all other perks, amounted to $300,000. My lifestyle changed from one of financial struggle to one of more financial freedom. I traveled extensively across the United States each week and enjoyed elite status with airlines, hotels, and car rental companies. My frequent business trips accumulated so many miles that we rarely paid for family vacations out of our own pockets.

On the surface, I had achieved the epitome of success, fulfilling the expectations instilled in me throughout my upbringing: attend college, secure a lucrative job, amass wealth, and find happiness. However, I soon discovered that this seemingly ideal life came at a significant cost.

The constant demands of my career meant I was perpetually away from my family, often for weeks at a time. I missed countless birthdays, little league games, first steps, milestones, and holidays. Despite an inner voice urging me to slow down and prioritize my family, I remained driven by the belief that this was the necessary sacrifice for providing a comfortable life for my loved ones.

Packing for my next business trip often elicited tears from my boys. They'd repeatedly ask why I couldn't stay home and why I had to leave so frequently. I could also sense the strain my constant absences put on my relationship with Jessica. Not only did she face loneliness, but she shouldered the bulk of parenting responsibilities in my absence. I even have a vivid memory of four-year-old Mason clinging tightly to my leg, pleading with me not to go on another work trip.

The truth was, I was miserable and depressed. I felt trapped in gilded handcuffs, unable to comprehend my deep unhappiness. I even questioned my sanity, justifying my situation by reminding myself that anyone would be envious of my job.

The crux of the issue was that my career was misaligned with my core values and life purpose. I yearned to be present for my family, to be home every night, and to witness their daily lives unfold.

My moral compass relentlessly reminded me that my primary roles were those of husband and father. Every missed milestone, whether big or small, gnawed at my conscience. Boarding planes knowing I'd miss another talent show, game, or birthday became unbearable. Money held no value; I felt like I was selling my soul for a hefty paycheck.

I felt trapped because I was the sole breadwinner, and my demanding job allowed Jessica to stay home with the boys. The thought of leaving such a high-paying position seemed ludicrous.

However, throughout my life, my true passion had always been to help men, husbands, and fathers create fulfilling relationships at home. Looking back, I now realize (and always have) that I desired the same for myself. When I launched *The Dad Edge Podcast* and wrote my first book in 2015, I knew I had found my purpose and passion.

By the grace and blessings of God, The Dad Edge has evolved into a global movement over the past several years. It has become my full-time career and organization, allowing me to pursue work that ignites my passion while serving a greater purpose.

When it comes to raising our children, we naturally want to shield them from hardships. We desire their lives to be fulfilling and free from financial worries. We also want them to pursue their passions. However, many of us believe that these two aspirations cannot coexist. We often resign ourselves to pursuing unfulfilling work to secure a decent living. Some even experience guilt and shame for earning a living through their passions, having internalized the message that work is inherently separate from fulfillment.

I firmly believe that as technology advances and opportunities expand, individuals can increasingly make a good living by aligning their work with their passions. The question now becomes: How do we create an environment that encourages our children to explore and discover their own purpose and passions? Furthermore, how can they bridge the gap between purpose and financial independence? As fathers, we can actually help create this environment where our kids feel safe to explore their wildest dreams, their deepest ambitions, and highest hopes. Buckle up tight, because that is exactly what's next.

DIVINE LIGHTS: *NURTURING ASPIRATIONS AND GUIDING GROWTH*

The journey of fatherhood holds a unique privilege in guiding children through life's paths. Prayer emerges as a powerful tool for dads to accomplish this. They transcend mere spirituality, offering a sacred space where values are instilled and the bond between fathers and children can deepen. By intentionally seeking guidance through prayer, fathers demonstrate that some paths are best navigated with the support of something greater.

Amidst the daily hustle of family life, the habit of dads praying with their children becomes a cornerstone of their relationship. It extends beyond mere words, creating a safe haven where emotions are shared and a sense of direction is sought. In today's fast-paced and often overwhelming world, carving out time for shared prayer serves as an anchor, fostering connection and strengthening the foundation of trust between fathers and their children. Through these shared moments of prayer, dads not only impart a sense of right and wrong but also instill the importance of seeking wisdom from beyond, equipping their children with the strength to face life's challenges.

Initiate your prayers by seeking guidance and purpose for your children. Implore God's wisdom and discernment to understand the unique plan for each individual child. Often overlooked in our eagerness to identify signs and breadcrumbs of our own purpose, this step is crucial in nurturing their individual paths.

Once you've anchored your prayers in seeking guidance and purpose for your children, the next step is to cultivate an atmosphere of gratitude. Encourage your children to express thankfulness for the opportunities, challenges, and even the setbacks they encounter. Gratitude fosters a positive mindset and helps them recognize the valuable lessons embedded in life's twists and turns. Emphasize the importance of appreciating both the big and small blessings during this shared time of prayer. By instilling a habit of gratitude, you're not only shaping their perspective but also nurturing resilience, teaching them to find silver linings even in the face of adversity. This practice can become a powerful tool for personal growth, empowering your children to navigate life with a grateful heart.

As you continue to pray with your children, guide them in focusing on their strengths and talents. Encourage them to seek God's guidance in understanding and developing the unique gifts bestowed upon them. In a world that often emphasizes comparison and competition, it's crucial for children to recognize their individual strengths. Use this time of prayer to foster self-awareness and confidence in their abilities. By acknowledging and celebrating their talents, you're helping to build a foundation of self-esteem that will empower them to navigate challenges and contribute positively to the world around them. This intentional focus on strengths reinforces the idea that each child is uniquely equipped to fulfill their purpose in the grand tapestry of life.

One of the most enriching aspects of parenthood is the opportunity to pray with our children and seek guidance as we navigate the complexities of life. Praying together accomplishes two significant goals. First, it instills in our children the practice of asking for guidance through prayer. By modeling this behavior, we demonstrate the essence of prayer for guidance. Second, it encourages both us, as parents, and our children to actively identify our passions and areas of interest. This shared pursuit fosters a state of curiosity and appreciation as we explore the world's vast array of possibilities.

Here are a few examples of prayers you can share with your children:

Guidance and Purpose

"Dear God, we are deeply grateful for this precious time together. We pray for [child's name], seeking your guidance and illuminating their path in life. Help them discern the unique plan you have for them. May they confidently walk the path you have paved, knowing that your wisdom lights their way. Amen."

Cultivating Gratitude

"Heavenly Father, we approach you with hearts filled with gratitude. Today, we express our deepest appreciation for the opportunities, challenges, and even setbacks that enrich our lives. Help us recognize the valuable lessons embedded in every twist and turn. Guide [child's name] to cultivate a positive mindset by appreciating both the grand and the subtle blessings we encounter. In gratitude, we find strength. Amen."

Focusing on Strengths and Talents

"God, we are eternally grateful for creating [child's name] with unique strengths and talents. As we pray together, help them understand and develop these gifts you have bestowed upon them. Guide us in recognizing and celebrating their abilities. May [child's name] grow in self-awareness and confidence, knowing they are uniquely equipped to make positive contributions to the world. Amen."

Teaching Prayer for Guidance

"Dear Lord, we cherish this time to pray together as a father and child. Today, we lift our hearts seeking your guidance. Reveal the paths we should take and teach us to earnestly seek your wisdom through prayer. By doing so, may [child's name] learn the importance of seeking your guidance in all aspects of life. Keep us both curious and appreciative as we explore the world's boundless opportunities. Amen."Praying with our kids is an experience that connects us on such a deep level. It's a way we can speak words out loud together in the presence of Christ. God is always listening to us and desiring a connection with Him. Just as our heavenly Father listens to us, another beautiful gift we can give our children is listening to them.

DREAMS UNLEASHED: *ENCOURAGING AMBITIONS WITH ACTIVE LISTENING*

As we journey through life, we are often guided by the expectations and advice of others. This can lead to a tendency to steer our children toward conventional paths, subtly pushing them away from their own aspirations. However, nurturing their emotional well-being and fostering a strong parent-child connection hinges on actively listening to their hopes and dreams.

When we engage wholeheartedly in conversations about their aspirations, we cultivate a supportive environment that encourages them to embrace their authentic selves. This open dialogue fosters trust and conveys to our children that their thoughts and dreams are valued. By attentively listening to their hopes, we gain valuable insights into their passions and ambitions, empowering us to guide and support them in pursuing meaningful endeavors.

Furthermore, actively listening to our children's hopes and dreams contributes to the development of their self-esteem and confidence. Feeling heard and understood instills a sense of validation and affirmation, empowering children to believe in their capabilities. This positive reinforcement lays the foundation for resilience and a willingness to confront challenges, knowing they have a supportive ally who genuinely cares about their aspirations. In turn, this active listening not only strengthens the parent-child bond but also helps children cultivate a healthy sense of self, enabling them to navigate life's complexities with a greater sense of purpose and determination.

My eldest son, for instance, harbored a long-held dream of becoming a police officer. From a young age, he envisioned himself as a protector of the innocent, a beacon of hope amidst adversity. During my early parenting days, I felt compelled to share my own perspectives, highlighting the potential challenges associated with a career in law enforcement. I would often caution him, painting a picture of the risks and sacrifices involved.

However, upon reflection, I realized that my approach was counterproductive. Instead of fostering curiosity and connection, I had inadvertently shifted the focus to my own concerns, overshadowing his aspirations. When our children confide in us about their hopes and dreams, they present us with an opportunity to delve deeper into their visions, to truly understand the driving force behind their aspirations. It is a chance to demonstrate unwavering support and engagement in their life's journey.

Don't get me wrong: there is a valid reason we point out the potential challenges and downsides of their dreams. We don't do it because we're negative or want to dampen their spirits. We do it out of love, seeking to protect them from potential mistakes and setbacks. It stems from a good place, but it doesn't have the long-term effect we desire on the relationship. It doesn't foster the one thing we crave most—connection.

I regret the message I conveyed to my son for so many years. Instead, I should have embraced his passion and desire to be a protector and a hero. My approach should have been (and is now) to celebrate the incredible qualities that being a police officer embodies. Children, by their very nature, are boundless explorers, thinking big without limitations. Sometimes we inadvertently instill limiting beliefs in them instead of nurturing their imaginative thinking. Even if we don't fully agree with their chosen path, we can encourage them to explore it nonetheless. We can join them on the magical journey of their minds and hearts.

In essence, the significance of actively listening to our children's hopes and dreams extends far beyond mere communication; it's the cornerstone of a strong parent-child relationship. By attentively listening to their aspirations, we forge a deep, emotional connection that forms the foundation of a healthy and trusting bond. This connection extends beyond the immediate dialogue, creating an enduring sense of understanding and support that becomes the scaffolding upon which our children can construct the framework of their futures.

In embracing our children's dreams, we not only affirm their sense of self-worth but also cultivate an environment where they feel safe to explore and express their innermost desires. This shared journey of listening and understanding becomes a powerful catalyst for fostering resilience, instilling confidence, and nurturing a profound sense of belonging. As we actively engage in their hopes and dreams, we not only sow the seeds for their personal growth but also contribute to the cultivation of a relationship that withstands the test of time—a relationship built on mutual respect, love, and an unwavering commitment to seeing our children thrive in the fullness of their potential.

SOULFUL SYNERGY: *BALANCING DISCIPLINE WITH CONTROLLED CHAOS*

Guiding and supporting your children, instead of imposing your own expectations, is pivotal. Allow them the freedom to explore various paths and make their own choices.

As we journey with our kids, discovering what they want to do with their lives and what they are passionate about, let's be more of a guide. That means accompanying them with a compass of curiosity and appreciation. It's an approach that involves more asking and less telling, and subtly pointing out potential pitfalls without dominating the conversation.

Consider my own upbringing, where my mom emphasized the importance of going to college and getting a job that pays the bills. This is a common experience for many of us. Often, we may have disregarded our parents' advice, humorously thinking,

"There's Mom being Mom again!" Providing guidance is necessary, as evidenced by our heavenly Parent, who sent the only Son to guide and set an example for us. God gave us the gift of free will, a gift our children also have. Besides, despite our warnings, our kids will ultimately make their own decisions.

What if we engaged our children with insightful questions and listened to their answers, rather than telling them what we think they should do? By asking more questions, we can effectively help them think critically as they explore their passions.

What would it have looked like if instead of my mom telling me all the reasons not to go into the health and wellness industry, she could have asked questions to get me thinking about things a bit deeper? She could have asked questions like: "Oh wow! What a cool field you are pursuing! Do you by chance know what your options will be once you graduate? Do you know what jobs are available and what they pay? What do you think you would enjoy about that field the most? What do you think will be the most challenging about that field? What are your thoughts on starting your own company or working for someone else?" Then for her to really listen to my responses without the agenda of warning me off my path, and me tuning her out. These questions would have had me thinking about these things much earlier on. I might have stuck with it or I might have changed things up. In the end, those questions would have gotten me thinking and I would have viewed her as more of a guide instead of someone who was trying to crush my dreams.

Similarly, I realized I was following the same pattern with my son. I thought I was doing right by highlighting all the potential issues. Yet, a more encouraging stance would have been, "Wow! You are truly courageous! That job requires a kind of bravery many don't have, and that's something I see in you. What do you think you'd enjoy most about it? What are your concerns or fears? Do you know the salary range for a police officer? If you could design the perfect workday, what would it include? What if you pursued a career based purely on your passion, regardless of the income?" Such questions are not only about understanding our children better but also about building stronger connections and trust with them. They also guide them to think critically about their dreams and aspirations.

A WORLD OF WONDERS: *PROVIDING OPPORTUNITIES TO EXPLORE*

Expose your children to a variety of experiences, including cultural, educational, and volunteer opportunities. These experiences can help broaden their horizons and reveal potential areas of interest.

Our kids are forever changing, especially when they are little. Truth be told, so are we. When it comes to finding our purpose and passion, our areas of interest can shift depending on our age, life experience, and season. The average human being will change careers five to seven times over their lives. In fact, 30 percent of adults in the workforce will find a new job every twelve to fifteen months. As for our kids, their minds can change by the day. Our job as dads is to give them exposure to as many experiences as possible that they are interested in.

As parents, our job is to help our kids figure out what they enjoy and what they want to do in life. Kids change a lot, and that's normal. Adults change too, especially when it comes to their passions and dreams. Some people take a long time to decide what they want to do, and that's okay. For our kids, their interests can change quickly, almost every day. So, as dads, our role is to encourage them to try different things and experiences to discover what they enjoy and what they're interested in. This way, we help them learn and uncover what makes them happy.

It's always a good idea for our kids to try something new, whether to find out if they love it or realize it's not for them. Many of us introduce our kids to sports, an easy and effective way to expose them to different experiences. But what if we also encouraged our kids to explore what they are curious about for their purpose and passion? It might not be common, but imagine if our kids could shadow a profession they are interested in?

My oldest son (the one who wanted to be a police officer when he was little) is now seventeen years old. He wanted to be a police officer as a young boy, but over the years, his mind has changed many times. Now, he is passionate about becoming an entrepreneur and opening his own gym. He wants to create a gym that offers not just fitness training but also teaches MMA, BJJ, Krav Maga, kickboxing, and boxing. In his words: "I am passionate about creating a place where people can not only get fit but also learn to defend themselves and those they care about."

Ethan knows firsthand what it's like to feel bullied. As a young boy, he was smaller than most of his peers and sometimes became a target for bigger kids who liked to push others around. These experiences taught him the real feeling of helplessness and the importance of knowing how to protect oneself. Over the years, Ethan has not only caught up with his peers in size but also in confidence. He has developed a deep love for wrestling, a sport that is much more to him than just pins and takedowns. Wrestling has given Ethan valuable knowledge, skills, and a newfound confidence, which he is passionate about sharing. He dreams of creating a place where people can come together to learn these life skills. Ethan firmly believes that everyone should have the knowledge to defend themselves and their loved ones.

How inspiring is that? Ethan plans to shadow a successful local gym owner and visit a martial arts studio to gain as much insight as possible. This way, he can combine the best of both worlds under one roof. Encouraging our children to take such proactive steps is immensely beneficial. Ethan's approach to thoroughly understanding the business aspects before jumping in with his own resources is a smart and cost-effective strategy. All of this because of providing a kid with some opportunities to explore what they are interested in.

THE ORIGINS OF VIRTUE: *CULTIVATING THEIR ETHICAL AND MORAL LANDSCAPES*

Iinstilling values in our children is akin to gifting them a compass for their life's journey. These discussions lay the bedrock for understanding what truly matters in life and why. Values serve as a family's moral GPS, guiding us in making sound decisions and treating others with respect. When we engage in value-driven conversations, we cultivate a shared language that empowers our kids to navigate life's complexities, discerning between right and wrong. This dialogue isn't about imposing our beliefs but about nurturing our children's moral compass, empowering them to make choices aligned with the principles we cherish as a family.

Furthermore, discussing values with our kids fosters a sense of belonging and identity. It's an opportunity to convey the core beliefs that define our family unit. By openly sharing our values, we reinforce a connection that transcends mere biology; it's about being part of a shared mission. As parents, we play a pivotal role in shaping the moral foundation of our children, and these conversations ensure that our values are not just assumed but consciously embraced. Through these discussions, we equip our kids with the tools to navigate the world with integrity, empathy, and a clear sense of what it means to be a responsible and compassionate member of society.

Encourage open discussions about values and principles that hold significance in your family. Introduce them to the Christian values that guide your life and encourage them to reflect on how their values align with their life's purpose.

Here are a few values that might facilitate discussions with your kids as they pursue their dreams. These have been integral to our family for quite some time. I've noticed over the years that they have been excellent launching pads for discussion.

Integrity: Honesty and truthfulness are fundamental Christian values. In business, this translates to transparency in all dealings, including financial transactions and communication with customers, employees, and stakeholders.

Justice and Fairness: Christians are called to treat others justly and with fairness. This involves paying fair wages, pricing products and services equitably, and ensuring that all stakeholders are treated with respect and dignity.

Compassion: Compassion and empathy are central to the Christian faith. In business, this means understanding and considering the needs and concerns of employees, customers, and the community at large.

Stewardship: Christians often view themselves as stewards of the resources entrusted to them by God. In business, this translates to responsible and sustainable resource management, environmental consciousness, and a commitment to minimizing waste.

Service: The Christian value of service can be applied to business by focusing on meeting the needs of customers and the community. This includes providing quality products and services that enhance the well-being of others.

Respect for Human Dignity: Every individual is created in the image of God in Christianity. This belief should lead to a commitment to treating all employees and stakeholders with respect and dignity, regardless of their background, race, or beliefs.

Humility: Christian humility calls for recognizing one's limitations and understanding that success is not solely the result of one's efforts but is often influenced by external factors. In business, this means acknowledging the contributions of others and seeking guidance when necessary.

Generosity: The principle of giving is a significant aspect of Christian faith. In business, this can involve philanthropy, charitable donations, and a commitment to giving back to the community.

Ethical Leadership: Christian values emphasize the importance of ethical leadership. Business leaders are encouraged to lead by example, maintaining high moral and ethical standards, and setting a positive tone for the organization.

Forgiveness and Reconciliation: Christianity teaches forgiveness and reconciliation. In business, this means being open to resolving conflicts and addressing grievances with employees, partners, or customers in a spirit of forgiveness and reconciliation.

Prayer and Guidance: Seeking guidance from God through prayer and spiritual reflection is a Christian practice. In business, individuals may seek divine guidance in making important decisions and navigating ethical dilemmas.

Honest Communication: Christians are called to speak the truth in love. In business, this means maintaining clear, honest, and respectful communication with employees, customers, and other stakeholders.

These values can provide a robust ethical and moral framework for our kids' lives in a way that is not only profitable for conducting business but also contributes positively to the well-being of the wider community.

Chapter V
Developing
Compassionate
Communication

n the tapestry of family life, communication serves as the thread that weaves everything together. However, this vital element often falls prey to the strains of modernity—fraying, unraveling, or even vanishing altogether, leaving families grappling with misunderstandings, misinterpretations, and missed opportunities for growth and connection. As Christian fathers, we are entrusted with the responsibility of leading our children with unwavering love, empathy, and wisdom. But how can we effectively guide our kids when we ourselves have not been equipped with the necessary tools of authentic communication?

The reality is that many of us have navigated our formative years without receiving formal instruction in the art of meaningful communication. We observed the interactions between our parents, perhaps unconsciously absorbing and replicating their patterns, both positive and negative. We internalized the unspoken rules and expectations that governed communication within our homes, often without critically evaluating their efficacy.

The consequences of this communication deficit can be profound. As we embark on our own journeys as fathers, we find ourselves entangled in the same communication quagmires that once plagued our families. This experience is far from uncommon; we are not alone in facing these challenges. Yet, by acknowledging these obstacles, we also hold the power to transform our families through the acquisition and practice of effective communication principles.

In this chapter, we will examine the stumbling blocks that impede open and honest conversations within families. We will uncover the secret to effective communication in fostering loving and trusting households. We will also equip you with the tools and insights necessary to unlock the transformative power of communication, enabling you to cultivate understanding, connection, and spiritual growth within your family. Together, we will embark on a journey, not only as fathers but as students of our own stories, excavators of buried emotions, and menders of generational divides, paving the way for open dialogues that will echo through generations.

TRUTH WITH TENDERNESS: *BALANCING HONESTY AND EMPATHY*

Many of us avoid expressing our true selves or being honest with others. This happens within our family units and beyond, in friendships, acquaintances, coworker relationships, and even with extended relatives. Speaking our truth can be frightening. There are several reasons why we avoid truth-telling and honesty, but one significant reason stems from our upbringing. So many adults, who are now parents, grew up in homes and families where honesty was met with shame, pain, blame, and guilt.

As children, many of us were punished when we were truthful with our own parents, siblings, or friends. Speaking our truth can manifest in a few different ways. One is when we speak up after doing something wrong or dishonest. This is extremely difficult for most of us because there is usually a price to pay, and it takes time to earn back trust in relationships. As a result, we avoid telling the truth. When we don't feel the freedom to speak our truth, it inevitably creates a significant divide in our most cherished relationships. We can even harbor emotional resentment within these relationships because we don't feel the freedom to be our most authentic selves. If you are reading these pages, you know that this is not what you want for your family. You want to create an environment where your children and partner feel comfortable sharing anything with you. You want to be the "go-to person" for those you love, a space where they can be their most authentic selves. It's a beautiful gift to give to our families, and you are likely replicating the sense of safety you craved as a child.

The question then becomes, how do we achieve this? Our God embodies mercy, forgiveness, and redemption, and truly desires our liberation from shame and guilt. God wants us to live our most authentic lives, with Christ as our foundation. We cannot effectively serve as warriors for Christ if we are constantly weighed down by shame and guilt, and, ultimately, dishonesty.

REVERBERATIONS OF OURSELVES: *MODELING EFFECTIVE FAMILY INTERACTIONS*

I understand that reading "lead by example" again might sound repetitive, as it's been emphasized throughout these pages. But bear with me, as it's a crucial concept. If we want to create an environment where others feel comfortable expressing their truth without fear, we must be willing to do it ourselves. The most valuable life lessons for our families are not taught; they are caught. Our children are far more perceptive than we give them credit for. They can detect inconsistencies between our words and actions. They are constantly assessing whether our "audio" matches our "video." Most of our children won't explicitly point this out, but trust me, they notice everything.

In our family, we have a simple yet powerful code regarding honesty: "Your honesty and accountability are celebrated and never punished." When a family member has something to share about any wrongdoing, they won't be met with shame, blame, pain, or guilt. While we will have discussions about improvement and potential consequences, you will always be met with love and praise for your courage to speak up. The same principle applies to providing honest feedback to someone not living up to their full potential. In our family, we speak truth and offer feedback out of love when we see someone falling short of their potential. Again, this approach is always rooted in love and support.

OPEN HEARTS, OPEN MINDS: *ENCOURAGING AUTHENTICITY AND TRUST*

About a year ago, I took my eldest son, Ethan, to the season finale of *The Chosen* season 3 at the movie theater and then to dinner. Jessica and I believe in taking our boys on one-on-one dates as often as possible. There's always something magical that happens when we can connect with our boys individually. They're not sharing time with their other three brothers, there aren't any distractions, and it's always a good opportunity for deeper conversation and connection.

Over dinner, I sensed that Ethan was holding onto something and was even a bit overwhelmed. After noticing it throughout the night, I trusted my intuition and decided to ask him about it.

"Hey, buddy, I want to ask you something, and I have no idea what answer you're going to give me. I have no agenda here, and I'm not trying to get you to tell me something you think I might already know. Is there something you want to share with me that you think I might not understand or something you've been holding back?" I asked curiously.

As soon as that question dropped, I could see it in his body language. He took a deep breath and looked off to the side for a moment. After pausing for a few seconds, he said, "Yeah, Dad, actually there is something going on."

"Tell me more. What's on your mind? I'm all ears," I said in a warm and inviting tone of voice.

He took another deep breath and started to speak. "Dad, you remember a few weeks ago when I stayed home from school for four days because I was really sick?"

"Of course," I responded.

"Dad, I have seven missing assignments right now and two Fs in two different classes. I fell behind when I was sick, and I haven't been able to catch up. Every time I get a few of the missing assignments done, I get three or four more. I get those done, and then I get three or four more. I can't catch up no matter what I do. I feel like I'm on a treadmill. It's my sophomore year of high school, and I don't want my grades to suffer, especially when I'm trying to keep my GPA up for college."

I smiled because I could tell as he unpacked that, the stress of carrying that weight was visibly lifting. It was almost like fresh oxygen was being put back into his body, and he wasn't holding onto such a heavy burden anymore.

"Wow! I bet that took some courage to say that out loud, huh? Tell me more," I said warmly, inviting him to continue.

I could tell those inviting words landed well for him because he jumped right in. "Dad, I'm so stressed out. I feel like I'll never catch up. I'm working a ton, and I feel like I'm on a treadmill going nowhere," he said a bit more freely.

I smiled and looked into his eyes with pride. "Ethan, I really appreciate you having the courage to talk to me about this and trusting me. This situation sounds frustrating, buddy. I remember being in your shoes, and truth be told, I still get into those situations where I fall behind. It is stressful, and it does happen, especially when we get sick. Ethan, I remember last semester you got COVID, and you were out of school for a full week. I believe you were faced with a similar dilemma of missing assignments and grades starting to fall," I said.

"Yeah, Dad, that did happen," he agreed.

"Ethan, the story I'm telling myself is that you got through that just fine. Do you remember what you did to get through it?" I asked.

He suddenly looked brighter and reassured. Almost like there was a beaming light bulb above his head.

"I actually do! I had one F and several missing assignments. If I remember correctly, I stayed up about an hour later than normal getting stuff done. I woke up thirty minutes earlier to knock a few things out before school. During lunch for three straight days, I went into the auditorium and did my work without distractions because no other students were in the auditorium during lunch. It took me those full three days, but I got it all done," he said confidently.

I smiled back. We both knew what had just happened. He knew exactly what needed to be done.

"Ethan, sounds like to me you've got the plan to make this happen," I said warmly.

"I do! That's what I'm going to do," he said with all confidence.

I'm happy to say he followed the plan and got done with everything in two days. The grades came up, and all missing assignments were completed. No shame.

For anyone wondering why I didn't impose additional consequences, it's because Ethan was already facing natural consequences for his actions:

- He had to sacrifice sleep by going to bed later to catch up on schoolwork.
- He had to forgo other activities he would have preferred to do in the evenings to focus on his studies.
- He had to wake up earlier than usual to get some schoolwork done before starting the school day.
- He had to eat lunch alone in the auditorium, missing out on socializing with his friends, to complete his assignments.

I could have easily resorted to shaming and guilting him. I could have bombarded him with words like, "We don't accept Fs in this family. What's wrong with you? Everything is off-limits until you complete those assignments and bring those grades up. We don't tolerate failure in this family." Perhaps that's how you were raised, and many of our generation were raised that way. However, how effective would that approach have been in that moment? Ethan would likely have walked away from that conversation feeling even worse about himself than he already did. He might not have even attempted to create a plan to get back on track and might have simply given up, believing his efforts were futile. Additionally, he would have made a mental note that his father is not someone he can turn to with his problems. That's not the kind of environment I want to create in my home, and chances are you don't either.

I'm not suggesting that this approach should be used every time our children make poor decisions or act impulsively. However, I believe this approach is more effective and can be applied in 80 to 90 percent of situations.

When we reflect on it, we realize that this is how God interacts with us. God is forgiving and merciful, and desires for us to embody those same qualities as much as possible.

COMPASSION'S EMBRACE: *WHAT MERCY MEANS AS A SPIRITUAL FATHER*

The concept of God's forgiveness and the call to repentance is deeply interwoven with the essence of divine love and mercy. God's readiness to forgive is a testament to a divine and infinite compassion for humanity, affirming that despite our flaws and missteps, a steadfast source of grace is always available, transcending our limitations. This forgiveness hinges not on our flawlessness but on our sincere repentance and commitment to amend our ways. This focus on repentance highlights God's desire for a transformative relationship with us, turning our acknowledgment of faults into a springboard for personal growth and spiritual rejuvenation.

Moreover, the call to repentance invites us into a profound reconciliation with God. It recognizes our human tendency to err and God's generous offer of redemption. Rooted in love, God's call to repentance aims to see us flourish and lead lives enriched by God's teachings. It suggests that through heartfelt repentance, we open ourselves to the life-changing power of God's forgiveness, liberating ourselves from guilt and fostering a rejuvenated bond with the divine. Essentially, God's willingness to forgive and the call to repentance illuminate the perpetual nature of divine love and the chance for spiritual rebirth available to all seekers.

Several Bible verses vividly illustrate this:

Psalm 103:8–12: "The Lord is compassionate and gracious, slow to anger, abounding in love. He will not always accuse, nor will he harbor his anger forever; he does not treat us as our sins deserve or repay us according to our iniquities. For as high as the heavens are above the earth, so great is his love for those who fear him; as far as the east is from the west, so far has he removed our transgressions from us."

Isaiah 1:18: "Come now, let us settle the matter," says the Lord. "Though your sins are like scarlet, they shall be as white as snow; though they are red as crimson, they shall be like wool."

1 John 1:9: "If we confess our sins, he is faithful and just and will forgive us our sins and purify us from all unrighteousness."

Ephesians 1:7: "In him we have redemption through his blood, the forgiveness of sins, in accordance with the riches of God's grace."

Micah 7:18–19: "Who is a God like you, who pardons sin and forgives the transgression of the remnant of his inheritance? You do not stay angry forever but delight to show mercy. You will again have compassion on us; you will tread our sins underfoot and hurl all our iniquities into the depths of the sea."

Psalm 86:5: "You, LORD, are forgiving and good, abounding in love to all who call to you."

Colossians 3:13: "Bear with each other and forgive one another if any of you has a grievance against someone. Forgive as the Lord forgave you."

These verses emphasize God's willingness to forgive the sins of those who come with a repentant heart. They offer reassurance and encouragement to all who seek God's forgiveness and grace.

THE PREPARED HEART: *FACING TOUGH CONVERSATIONS WITH GRACE*

Sometimes, we must brace ourselves for honest feedback that might be difficult to hear, or we may need to deliver such feedback, despite our reluctance. This is crucial for maintaining healthy family dynamics and genuine connections, as it's essential to share the truth lovingly.

Reflecting on a recent personal experience, I encountered this very situation. I faced a hard truth, which was quite disheartening. Truth can be challenging; it often feels overwhelming, akin to an onslaught. At times, it's like confronting an infection—painful and overpowering. Yet, by embracing the truth, we can effectively address the "infection," applying the "antibiotics" of understanding and action. Over time, with proper attention, the issue heals, leading to a happier, healthier state. Likewise, truth in relationships works the same way. Ignoring issues or withholding truth is like neglecting an infection—it only worsens and can lead to severe consequences.

Currently, I'm in a particularly demanding phase of life. I'm working against a tight deadline for this book, managing over one hundred subcontractors, serving nearly a thousand clients, and raising four young men. My marriage requires my utmost attention, not to mention my personal commitments to my faith and health. Amidst this whirlwind, my schedule has never been more packed or demanding.

A few days ago, a truth was shared with me by a close friend, someone I deeply respect. I had noticed our interactions diminishing over recent months. My texts were often met with brief responses or none at all, a stark contrast to our usual friendship dynamics. This change culminated in complete silence. Eventually, I confronted him about this noticeable shift, as it was out of character for both him and our relationship.

I reached for my phone and sent him a text: "Hey man, I'm puzzled about what's happening. I've tried reaching out several times but haven't heard back. I'm starting to wonder if I've done something wrong, or if you're just too busy, or if something else is going on."

It took a day for his reply to come through. The next morning, as I sat in my gym's parking lot at 6:30 a.m., his text arrived. Eager yet apprehensive, I opened the message, not expecting the contents that awaited me.

> Hey bro, just saw your text. So I will be honest. Something had kind of bugged me for a while. I felt like almost all the instances we spoke I felt a bit like "the light was on, but Larry wasn't home."

That I would send messages talking about various things. And either you would respond to about 25 percent of what I even talked about. Or when you did the messages were often short, even abrupt. Like a quick response but no questions my way or probing deeper. I vividly remember one time I sent you some detailed messages and your response was like one or two lines. No asking how I was or anything. I remember one time I even told you this. Because it was frustrating me. I said, dude, you don't reply to so much of what I say and at the time you said something like "I'm sorry, man, it's just been a busy WEEK." But that wasn't just an observation I had made that week, bro; it was something you do ALL the time. I even asked Vito once if he felt like at times it's like you just "weren't there" because I was wondering if it was just me being a sensitive snowflake. And he did say, he felt like you do that. (Don't tell him I told you as I don't want to throw him under the bus. He did say you have so much on your plate, etc.) All this to say, I do miss our connection man. But I really felt like often we would talk and you weren't there. And I think you KNOW it, that you have/were spread thin, that you have so many people you deal with and tend to. And I am telling you, man, with absolute certainty this has been going on for a LONG time, I just always bite my tongue. In a way, bro, I just didn't want to add to that more. And I have also gone through seasons in my life where I needed people around who I could sense were truly listening. All this to say. You are a great guy, massive heart. But I know you spread yourself too thin and then you can't give anyone the best version of you at all, bro. I just didn't want to add to that list. Love you, man, and I am here for you. I wasn't even sure if I should say all this because I'm a bit mentally tired right now and not really in the mood to have intense discussions, but I don't want to ghost you either as you and I both know we hate that shit. But you are diluting yourself down so much that you catch like 10 percent of a conversation and I don't even think you realize it. I love you, brother. Hope you can take this constructively.

Reading his words, my heart dropped. Part of me wanted to react defensively, to deflect or even to ignore the message. Another part wanted to shift the blame back to him, feeling like he was doing the same to me. But instead, I paused. I began to ponder if there was truth in his words. Questions flooded my mind: "How long has this been happening? Have others been affected by my actions? Could I have lost other relationships due to this behavior?" After reflecting, I came to appreciate his bravery in confronting me. He was risking our friendship and possibly igniting a conflict. His honesty required immense courage and wasn't easy. Yet, he cared enough about me to speak up, risking confrontation rather than silence. Avoidance would have only bred more resentment and distance, potentially ending our friendship without me ever understanding why. I might have dismissed it as another failed relationship, another person walking away, without recognizing my role. It could have been the untreated "infection" that ended our friendship.

Confronted with this hard truth, I reached out to other friends, inquiring if they had similar experiences with me. The unanimous response from those I love and trust was, "Yes. There is truth to that." I also turned to Jessica, and our sons Ethan (seventeen), Mason (fifteen), and Lawson (nine), asking if they felt the same way. Each one confirmed, "Yes. There is truth to that." My friends shared that they had observed this behavior for a while but hadn't voiced their concerns. Jessica noticed it months ago but didn't find it severe enough to bring up. This kind of response can be perilous for relationships, indicating a tolerance of poor behavior that hasn't yet reached a breaking point.

We can all agree that when a relationship deteriorates to such a level, the journey back to health is daunting. Like an untreated infection becoming septic, the healing process might require intensive care, such as hospitalization and long-term treatment. Nobody desires that outcome, and if you're reading this, you likely don't either. Ethan and Mason's feedback was hard to hear, but the most heart-wrenching came from Lawson, my nine-year-old. His innocent words and perspective brought me to tears. "Dad, sometimes when I talk to you, you don't seem to hear me. Sometimes, I feel like you're not really listening." Hearing this from my young son was crushing. I felt like a complete imposter, teaching other men about these issues while failing to apply them in my own life.

God teaches us that truth liberates us, even when it doesn't feel like a gift at the moment. He also shows us that shame keeps us hidden, preventing us from seeking forgiveness and working on mending what's broken.

You might be curious about how I reacted to all this honest feedback, as I faced the reality of these truths. Initially, my instinct was to defend myself, perhaps even find justifications. But deep down, I knew they were right. So, I accepted every bit of their feedback. I expressed gratitude to everyone for their honesty and bravery in speaking up. I couldn't bear the thought of remaining ignorant for even a day longer, continuing to unknowingly hurt those most important to me. As I write this, I am actively working on repairing these relationships. I'm grateful to have identified this issue early enough to prevent it from causing irreparable damage to my closest bonds.

This experience highlights an important lesson: when our loved ones have the courage to be honest with us, we need to take their words seriously. Before rushing to defend ourselves, or shifting the blame, it's crucial to reflect on the truth in their words and our role in the situation. If we find truth in their feedback, we should commend them for their courage to speak up, a path they could have easily avoided. Then, it's time to start the work of repairing what's been damaged.

These are lessons that are caught, not taught. If my goal is to raise individuals who can gracefully handle tough truths with love, I must exemplify this behavior myself. I can't expect them to develop this trait if I'm not leading by example.

KINDNESS IN CRITIQUE: *DELIVERING FEEDBACK WITH TENDERNESS*

Many have grown up in homes where words were often hurtful and negatively impacted relationships. Throughout my practice, I've encountered numerous clients raised in environments where "no news was good news," and communication mainly highlighted what was wrong, broken, or missing. This scenario is not only prevalent in many households but also in various workplace cultures.

The effects of this constant negativity and the "no news is good news" communication style are significant. Research has shown that children raised with predominantly negative feedback can face several challenges in adulthood. The following list, while possibly familiar to many, underscores the negative consequences of this approach.

Lower Self-Esteem

Receiving continuous negative or critical feedback, especially from family, can gradually erode a person's self-esteem and sense of self-worth. This often results in reduced confidence and a diminished sense of personal value. Naturally, we all aspire to raise confident, self-assured individuals who contribute positively to society.

Increased Stress and Anxiety

Frequent negative communication, such as criticism or harsh words, can foster a stressful family environment. This prolonged stress is a known contributor to anxiety and other mental health issues. Studies indicate that around 1 in 25 adults suffer from a serious mental disorder. The CDC reports that 13.2 percent of US adults are on antidepressants, a figure that doesn't include other medications like anti-anxiety drugs, antipsychotics, opioids, or substances such as alcohol and marijuana.[1]

Deterioration of Relationships

Harsh or unkind words can severely strain family relationships. Minor disagreements can escalate into conflicts, eroding trust and connection. Many of us have witnessed or experienced this breakdown in relationships firsthand.

Emotional Pain

Unkind or hurtful words can inflict deep emotional pain, often with long-lasting effects. Healing these emotional wounds requires time and effort and can significantly impact mental and emotional health. The old adage "sticks and stones may break my bones, but words will never hurt me" is now often

---

1. Debra J. Brody, MPH, and Qiuping Gu, MD, PhD, "Antidepressant Use Among Adults: United States, 2015–2018," *NCHS Data Brief*, no. 377 (September 2020), https://www.cdc.gov/nchs/data/databriefs/db377-H.pdf.

viewed with skepticism. It's widely recognized that words can leave profound, indelible marks on our hearts and minds.

Depression
Persistent negative communication can contribute to feelings of sadness and hopelessness, potentially leading to depression in some cases.

Negative Behavior Patterns
Children in environments lacking positive words often develop negative behaviors, like seeking validation externally, engaging in harmful activities, or struggling to build healthy relationships. Experts have long advised that children crave attention, whether positive or negative, and will accept either form. As they mature, these negative behaviors can become ingrained as their norm.

Communication Barriers
In families lacking supportive communication, members may hesitate to share their thoughts and feelings, leading to communication barriers. These barriers can prevent conflict resolution and deepen misunderstandings. Whether we've been the cause or on the receiving end, we've likely seen the impact of such barriers in our relationships.

Studies indicate that people, including children, respond more positively to praise for good behavior than to criticism for missteps.[2] It's important to clarify that this doesn't mean ignoring or enabling bad behavior. Rather, it suggests using encouraging words more and critical comments less. Personally, I aim for an 80/20 or 90/10 ratio of positive to negative feedback, though admittedly, I don't always hit the mark.

When praised or rewarded for desirable actions, children, and even adults, are more likely to repeat those behaviors. Receiving praise from superiors, peers, or family can boost us in the following ways:

Effectiveness of Praise

Praise has been shown to be a powerful motivator, enhancing effort, academic performance, and self-esteem in children. It often proves more effective in promoting desired behavior than punishment or criticism.[3]

Cultivating Intrinsic Motivation

Positive reinforcement, like praise, fosters intrinsic motivation in children. When they are commended for their efforts and achievements, they develop a

---

2. Gwen Dewar, PhD, "The Effects of Praise: 7 Evidence-Based Tips for Using Praise Wisely," Parenting Science, https://parentingscience.com/effects-of-praise/.

3. Elizabeth Gunderson et al., "Parent Praise to 1- to 3-Year-Olds Predicts Children's Motivational Frameworks 5 Years Later," *Child Development* 84, no. 5 (September 2013): 1526–41, doi:10.1111/cdev.12064.

genuine interest in activities, independent of external rewards or fear of punishment.

Building Self-Esteem

Praise and positive reinforcement play a vital role in developing a child's self-esteem and a healthy self-concept. Recognition of their achievements helps children feel valued and capable, fostering positive self-image and confidence.

Enhancing Parent-Child Relationships

A parenting style centered on praise and encouragement fosters strong parent-child relationships. Children feel more secure, supported, and loved when their efforts are recognized. Meeting children's needs to feel seen, heard, and safe is achievable through positive communication, deepening the parent-child bond.

While these principles are widely recognized in child psychology, the effectiveness of praise also depends on its delivery. Effective praise should be specific, sincere, and focused on effort and process, not just outcomes. Balancing constructive feedback with praise is recommended to help children recognize their strengths and areas for growth.

REFLECTIVE HONESTY: *EMBRACING TRUTH IN OURSELVES AND RELATIONSHIPS*

When it comes to utilizing praise and positive reinforcement with our children, recognizing their unique personalities and needs is crucial. A strategy that's effective for one child might not resonate as well with another, highlighting the importance of a customized approach.

A key point to consider, which I've personally reflected on, involves the balance of edification and realism in our interactions. While I lean toward a predominantly positive approach (80/20 or 90/10), it's important to clarify that not all my conversations with my kids are centered around edification. Discussions encompass various topics that aren't always about their decisions, school performance, or daily work ethic. I firmly believe in offering sincere positive feedback. Just as research has shown the benefits of positive reinforcement, it's also clear that excessive, insincere praise can be ineffective.[4] Over-praising can come across as disingenuous, leading children to question the sincerity of our feedback.

---

4. Ai Mizokawa, "Association Between Children's Theory of Mind and Responses to Insincere Praise Following Failure," *Frontiers in Psychology* 9, article 1684 (October 2018): doi:10.3389/fpsyg.2018.01684.

I recall a valuable discussion with Dan Peterson, founder of The Compass 4 Life, an LCPC and an advanced trainer for the Nurtured Heart Approach. Dan, who holds a master's degree in clinical psychology and is an expert in the Nurtured Heart Approach, shared insightful guidelines on our podcast about connecting and communicating effectively with children.[5] According to Dan, praise should be effective communication with our kids. Quite simply when we praise our kids:

> *It must be genuine.*
> Kids can sniff from a mile away if we are giving them lip service and don't truly mean what we say.

> *It must be specific (not just "you did good!").*
> Share details of what you saw or heard your kid did (or doing).

> *Never praise for outcomes alone.*
> While outcomes matter, the effort and journey are equally, if not more, important. Praise should link

---

5. Larry Hagner, "Stop Yelling and Start Connecting with Dan Peterson," February 17, 2023, *The Dad Edge Podcast*, episode 55, https://thedadedge.com/dan-peterson/.

to positive traits like kindness, honesty, work ethic, integrity, and bravery.

This approach ensures that praise not only feels real to our kids but also contributes meaningfully to their development and self-esteem.

My fifteen-year-old son, Mason, has been dedicated to football since third grade and is now in his seventh year. His commitment has involved not just skill but also immense dedication and effort. As a key player in his JV team, Mason excels as the starting center, the long snapper for PATs, a crucial member of the special teams for kickoff and return, and is often called upon as nose guard or linebacker for critical defensive plays. Additionally, he contributes to the varsity special teams.

Mason's coaches aptly describe him as "the Swiss army knife of the team," owing to his versatility and reliability in various positions. Despite his wide array of skills, Mason remains a humble player. He avoids showboating after significant plays and maintains respect for his opponents and teammates, embodying a quiet, stoic, yet formidable presence on the field. One consistent, remarkable behavior I've observed in him, unrelated to his game performance, is his sportsmanship. After making a big tackle, Mason consistently offers a helping hand to his opponent, sometimes even giving them a reassuring pat on the back. Witnessing such gestures is incredibly heartening.

I make it a point to acknowledge these qualities in Mason with specific, meaningful praise. While excelling in life's endeavors is important, fostering good character is paramount. So, my praise for Mason goes beyond his athletic performance. It sounds like this: "Mason, fantastic game today! I saw your hard work and dedication on the field. Your consistent practice, play study, disciplined training, and nutrition show your commitment. But what truly stood out was your act of helping your opponents up after a tackle. That's a sign of genuine character, humility, and sportsmanship. These are the qualities of a true athlete. Keep it up, Mason!"

This approach to praise is specific, heartfelt, and highlights positive character traits. As parents, especially fathers, we have the incredible opportunity to teach our children values like character, integrity, and honesty. This teaching goes well beyond mere words; it involves living out these values ourselves and recognizing them in our children's actions.

CHAPTER VI
A LEGACY OF LOVE

As I reflect on my twenty-year marriage with Jessica while writing this book, I recall my initial struggles with personal faith. Early on, I felt overwhelmed by it and distant from Christ, rationalizing this detachment in various ways. I believed I wasn't worthy of a relationship with Christ and I considered myself a sinner. The Bible seemed daunting to me; its teachings too abstract for modern-day relevance. In my conversations with other men over the years, I've noticed common themes around feeling overwhelmed by the notion of spiritual leadership in the family. Many felt daunted by the Bible and unsure of interpreting its scriptures. A frequent sentiment was not knowing where to start, which would then lead to inaction.

I, too, held these beliefs early in my marriage. Yet the truth is none of us are inherently worthy of

God's mercy, but love, grace, and forgiveness are still extended to us. We are called to be spiritual leaders in our families, much like the apostles, who felt unworthy yet were called upon to lead. Matthew, the tax collector, didn't feel worthy but still followed Jesus and became a key figure in the New Testament. We are all called to lead, but answering that call can be challenging.

Another reason for my initial reluctance was Jessica's deep faith. Often, she would go to church alone, as I didn't see the value in it, feeling "good enough" without a deeper spiritual connection. I thought of myself as a decent person—kind, law-abiding, a good father and husband, and a reliable provider. Looking back, I realize how naive and misguided those perceptions were.

Some fathers may not embrace spiritual leadership because they view themselves as "good enough" on a relative scale. If they aren't committing serious wrongs, they may feel they meet the criteria for a decent father. However, this overlooks the transformative role of spiritual leadership in nurturing a strong, connected family. Believing that avoiding negative actions is enough neglects the vital role of actively guiding the spiritual growth of their children. Without recognizing the enriching influence of spiritual leadership, fathers may miss opportunities to deepen and support their family's dynamics.

Societal expectations and common misconceptions about spiritual leadership often contribute to dads' hesitation. Many fathers may view the role as requiring an unattainable level of perfection or extensive religious knowledge. Overwhelmed or feeling inadequate, they might step back from their potential role as spiritual leaders. It's key to emphasize that spiritual leadership doesn't require perfection, but a sincere, humble effort to share values, engage in meaningful conversations, and build a sense of purpose and connection within the family. By dispelling these misconceptions, dads can understand the impactful role they can play in their family's spiritual development.

I also believe that the enemy prefers the passive believer, like my former self. The enemy isn't as focused on those who are disengaged, like I was, but rather on those actively engaged in their faith. If I could talk to myself twenty years ago, I would encourage stepping more actively into spiritual leadership. These past few years have been a learning curve for me, and I'm only beginning to understand what it means to have a close relationship with God, realizing there's so much more to explore in this journey.

In the years since embarking on this spiritual journey, I've noticed a significant reduction in my stress and anxiety levels. I've come to understand that life happens for me, not to me. Even in challenging times, I now see opportunities for spiritual growth. It's not always a smooth journey; indeed, some days are tough and filled with pain. Yet, it's important to remember that growth often comes with its share of discomfort. Sometimes the pain is sharp and the challenges daunting, while at other times, they're milder and more easily navigated.

In summary, the hesitancy of some fathers to assume a role as spiritual leaders, often due to a belief that they are "good enough" by merely avoiding serious wrongs, highlights a need for a new perspective. True spiritual leadership is less about avoiding negative actions and more about actively engaging in a process of continuous learning and personal growth. Embracing leadership as an ongoing journey allows fathers to realize that there's always room for personal and spiritual development.

Spiritual leadership isn't about attaining perfection, but about a commitment to continual learning and evolving with a willingness to share these insights with their families.

Understanding spiritual leadership as a continual learning process changes the narrative around sufficiency. Fathers, like all individuals, aren't expected to know everything. Instead, they are encouraged to embark on a journey of discovery, seeking wisdom, and creating a space where spiritual growth is a collective journey. By accepting that leadership is dynamic and evolving, fathers can move past the idea of needing to be perfect, focusing on the enriching experience of leading their families with love, empathy, and shared spiritual principles.

GRATITUDE IN THE ORDINARY: *FINDING JOY IN LIFE'S SIMPLE GIFTS*

At the core of building a resilient, compassionate family with lasting values is the role of dads in exemplifying strong faith. Fathers are pivotal in influencing their children's character and spiritual beliefs. A father's unwavering commitment to his faith acts as a guiding light, leading children toward a profound understanding of spirituality. This influence goes beyond mere religious practices; it encompasses demonstrating how faith shapes everyday actions, teaching children the value of moral integrity, empathy, and resilience against life's hurdles.

Moreover, when dads embody strong faith, they lay the groundwork for a family culture rich in shared beliefs and unity. Faith transforms into a collective strength, knitting the family together. Through this shared spiritual journey, dads inspire unity and purpose, creating an environment where children feel nurtured, valued, and part of something larger than themselves. A dad's strong faith echoes throughout the family, fostering a cohesive unit where values are not just taught but lived, and a shared purpose is embraced.

I can almost hear you saying, "Larry, you've mentioned this in every chapter." And yes, I reiterate it because its importance cannot be overstated. The values we wish to see in our families must be embodied by us. We can't expect our spouses and children to follow suit if they don't witness us living these values.

Addressing a common challenge, let's acknowledge that modeling strong faith is straightforward when life is easy. When our finances are stable, our health is good, our kids are thriving, and our marriages are strong, living our faith feels natural. However, it's during these comfortable times that we risk becoming complacent in actively demonstrating our faith.

Becoming too settled in our spiritual journey is akin to pausing in a swiftly flowing river—it's potentially hazardous. When we become too complacent and cease to seek spiritual growth, we risk missing out on the remarkable insights and experiences that are part of this path. Approach spirituality as an ongoing adventure; comfort might offer safety, but it can also mean missing out on the profound and enriching aspects of our faith.

It's essential to remain open to learning and evolving spiritually, as this keeps our connection with our beliefs vibrant and strong. Just as plants thrive with sunlight and nurturing, our spiritual well-being flourishes with fresh perspectives and challenges. Believing we have reached the pinnacle of understanding can be a pitfall. There is always more to uncover about our faith and ourselves. Continuously challenging ourselves ensures that our spiritual journey is dynamic, robust, and filled with new, enriching experiences. It's through this continuous exploration that we deepen our connection with the divine, enrich our spiritual lives, and gain a better understanding of the world.

When life is smooth and comfortable, it's easy to overlook expressing gratitude to God. This is where the ACTS (Adoration, Confession, Thanksgiving, and Supplication) framework can be particularly beneficial. It encourages us to pause and appreciate the remarkable blessings in our lives, keeping our focus on gratitude for the simple yet significant things.

Adoration allows us to stop and marvel at the Divine's greatness, cultivating a sense of wonder and respect. Confession goes beyond acknowledging errors; it's a truthful introspection of our faults, offering a chance for spiritual refinement. This practice keeps us grounded and sincerely connected to our faith.

Furthermore, Thanksgiving in ACTS serves as a potent reminder to recognize our blessings and express gratitude to God. Consciously acknowledging both the significant and minor gifts that enrich our lives fosters a spirit of gratefulness. This deliberate practice of gratitude strengthens our bond with the divine and encourages us to discover joy in everyday moments. The ACTS model provides a framework for continuously refocusing on the beauty in our lives, promoting a mindset of appreciation even in times of comfort and ease.

I know it might seem a bit obvious, but giving thanks for all the little things in our lives is important. Unless we make a conscious effort to notice them, they often slip under the radar. Simple things like the food on our table every night, the reliable car in our driveway, having a healthy body to play with our kids, or that unexpected hug from our seven-year-old for no reason other than they felt like giving it, and the warm smile from our spouses are all worth appreciating.

Delving deeper into gratitude for these seemingly ordinary aspects of our lives, we realize their transformative power. The food on our table is more than sustenance; it's a sign of the abundance we often overlook. The reliable car we drive is not just a means of transport; it represents the stability in our lives. The ability to physically engage with our children reflects the often unnoticed vitality of life.

The spontaneous hug from our child or a genuine smile from our spouse, without any particular reason, carries a deeper meaning. These moments are not just simple gestures; they are profound expressions of love and connection, enriching our life's experience. By consciously acknowledging and expressing gratitude for these small joys, we foster an attitude of appreciation for both the extraordinary and the everyday. This practice, in line with the ACTS model, helps us develop a heart full of gratitude, recognizing the beauty in the fabric of our daily lives.

It may seem small, but vocalizing these things out loud, especially in front of our family, is a powerful way to model gratitude. Additionally, praying for and with our children, expressing our thanks to God for the gift they are, enriches this practice. The more we pray with our children and involve them in our faith, the more beautiful the experience becomes.

BEYOND THE PEW: *THE RIPPLE EFFECT OF FAMILY FAITH*

Attending church with our children can be a powerful way for dads to actively contribute to their families' spiritual well-being. Studies consistently highlight the positive influence of regular religious attendance on family unity, moral development, and overall well-being. According to a National Survey of Children's Health study, children who attend religious services regularly are more likely to exhibit prosocial behaviors, like empathy and cooperation.[1] This suggests that the communal aspect of church attendance strengthens not only individual faith journeys but also cultivates valuable virtues that positively impact family dynamics.

Beyond the research, attending church with kids offers dads a unique opportunity to share core values and foster a sense of belonging. By worshipping together, fathers model the importance of spiritual practice, leaving a lasting impression on their children's faith journey. A *Journal for the Scientific Study of Religion* study found that children who regularly attend religious services with their fathers are more likely to carry these practices into adulthood. This emphasizes the crucial role fathers play in shaping their children's spiritual foundation and underscores

1. Carrie Spector, "Religiously Engaged Adolescents Demonstrate Habits That Help Them Get Better Grades, Stanford Scholar Finds," Standford Graduate School of Education, April 15, 2018, https://ed.stanford.edu/news/religiously-engaged-adolescents-demonstrate-habits-help-them-get-better-grades-stanford-scholar.

the enduring impact that regular church attendance can have on families.

As *The Citizen* study points out, if a father attends church regularly, regardless of the mother's attendance, between 66 percent and 75 percent of their children will likely attend as adults.[2] This surprised me years ago—it was both encouraging and a bit daunting! It wasn't until 2018 that I started attending weekly. Before that, it was sporadic. Weekly sometimes, monthly others. Honestly, sometimes it was seasonal or just on holidays.

Before I truly connected with faith, I admit I went through the motions. Church felt like a box I checked because I thought it was the right thing to do. Even then, I'd often drift off in my own thoughts. Looking back, I think it was for a few reasons. First, I didn't understand what I was hearing. Second, I questioned the importance of attending. And finally, I felt unworthy to be there.

The "not understanding" part boiled down to neglecting my relationship with faith. I didn't try to grasp it or spend time with it. So, of course, it made

---

2. David L. Chancey, "Dads, Your Presence in Worship Matters," *The Citizen*, June 21, 2020, https://thecitizen.com/2020/06/21/dads-your-presence -in-worship-matters/.

no sense! I was just going through the motions, not putting in any effort. It's like going to the gym once a week, eating poorly the rest of the time, and wondering why I wasn't getting fitter. Deepening our faith takes effort and dedication. Anything we excel at, we invest time and work into. I simply wasn't doing that.

When I believed that attending church was optional, I clearly underestimated its significance. This realization dawned on me gradually. My wife, a beacon of spirituality, has always been my inspiration to embrace a more divine way of life, to pray more, and to join her in church. For much of our marriage, she attended church while I stayed home with the kids, not grasping the full importance of my absence. This was a significant oversight on my part. Jessica deeply wished for me to share this spiritual journey with her. More than just a partner, she yearned for me to lead by example. Her dream was for me to guide our four young men toward a Christ-centered life and to nurture their bond with God. I must admit, the thought of leading in this way made me feel undeserving and unprepared. It seemed like an immense responsibility, one that I was unsure how to fulfill, fearful of making mistakes.

This perspective shifted when a spiritual mentor entered my life. In one of our Bible study sessions, he offered an insight that reshaped my thinking. "Larry," he said, "do you need to master everything before beginning? What if you approach this like any other learning experience in life? When you don't know something, you learn. Whether it's driving a car, fixing something, or cooking a new recipe, you learn and let your boys learn with you. So why not apply the same principle here? Lead by learning, show humility in not knowing everything, and embark on this journey with them. Isn't this what leading is all about?"

His words struck a chord with me. It became clear that I didn't need to know everything to be a role model. I could be a fellow learner alongside my sons. Together, we could embark on this spiritual journey, growing and learning as a family.

Suddenly, a weight lifted, and I felt empowered to take the first step. This was a revelation I never anticipated. (Side note: That's how you know you've got a true friend in your corner, someone who champions your potential with unwavering belief.

They see it sometimes even clearer than you do, more objectively and simply.) So, I dove in. Church became our family's new Sunday ritual, and the boys were all for it.

Over time, my eyes truly opened to wonders I hadn't noticed before. The dedicated weekly hour to connect with family in this spiritual space became a cherished haven. I reveled in the shared values and the sense of belonging that blossomed in this community. Even more, worshipping together forged an unexpected closeness, a beautiful tapestry woven from shared moments and weekly messages.

Those Sunday messages became springboards for captivating family conversations. We'd reflect, delve deeper, and fascinating insights would unfurl. Attending church as a family became an experience of profound connection, a space where we were not just present, but actively listening, absorbing, and growing together.

Now, I not only feel comfortable and worthy in that pew, but I thrive there. It's my sanctuary for learning and nurturing my faith, a space our family shares to cultivate our individual and collective journeys. And over the years, I've witnessed a blossoming in Jessica's love and connection with me, a depth I hadn't seen before. None of this was part of the plan, yet here we are, walking this path of faith, hand in hand, a family united.

EMBRACING IMPERFECTIONS: *A GUIDE TO AUTHENTIC SPIRITUAL LEADERSHIP*

Have you ever felt like you were put on the spot and had to come up with the perfect words? I know I have, especially when it came to praying with or for my kids. The pressure to have the "right" words felt immense, and it made things awkward early on. If you're reading this with a knowing smile, then you and I are in the same boat. We've both questioned ourselves, wondered if we were doing it right, and maybe even worried we sounded a little . . . unhinged. After all, prayer time is a vulnerable and authentic space. We share the deepest parts of our souls, and the fear of feeling like a fraud can really creep in.

I remember vividly one of the first times I prayed with my young sons. I felt this immense pressure not to sound like a total goof. I'd close my eyes, trying to make my words sound perfect. But then I'd open them to catch a glimpse of my little guy's face, trying not to crack up because he heard me stumble over my words. Not even my youngest was fooled! He could tell I was uncomfortable, and he found it hilarious to watch his dad squirm. It all boiled down to me thinking I had to be someone I wasn't: the perfect praying man.

Many dads can feel overwhelmed with praying out loud with their kids. It's that pressure to articulate our deepest thoughts and emotions in such a public way. Verbalizing our prayers feels vulnerable, like our words won't measure up to some expected spiritual eloquence. We feel like we need to convey this profound connection with the divine, and that pressure can be crushing, especially for those of us who aren't exactly wordsmiths or who are still figuring out our own faith journeys.

Many dads also feel the weight of setting the "right" example for their kids. Being their spiritual leader can be a heavy crown, adding to the pressure to craft the perfect prayer or deliver the perfect message. The fear of judgment, whether from their children or that imaginary image of the ideal spiritual leader, can turn prayer into a daunting performance. This pressure can breed feelings of inadequacy, making dads worry they'll fall short during these intimate moments.

But it wasn't until I embraced heartfelt prayer, letting God guide my words and actions, that the nervousness melted away. I released the need for control, perfection, and self-doubt. I remembered that God doesn't expect perfection; He wants connection and a growing relationship. It's like expecting a seven-year-old to talk like a grown-up—it's unrealistic and unnecessary. There's true strength in the humility of prayer, a vulnerability that connects us not only to the divine but also to our children on a deeper level.

True strength lies in acknowledging our own limitations and seeking guidance. When men pray with humility, they exhibit courage and authenticity, expressing gratitude, seeking forgiveness, and asking for guidance when needed.

This act is akin to being a strong leader who values collaboration and shared human experiences. Humble prayer is a recognition that we are all connected and part of something greater. Masculinity embraces authenticity, acknowledges imperfections, and wisely seeks divine assistance in life's journey.

Praying together, especially with our children, is an act of profound vulnerability and a rare opportunity for bonding. It's a moment where we, as fathers, can demonstrate our obedience to our Heavenly Father, and our commitment to being the earthly guardian of our children. In these moments of prayer, holding their hands, we express love and adoration toward God. We confess and release what burdens our hearts, express gratitude, and make meaningful requests. Above all, we seek guidance, peace, and the courage to share God's teachings.

THE POWER OF SURRENDER: *AN UNFORGETTABLE NIGHT OF PRAYER*

A heartwarming and unexpected moment happened recently that left me humbled. One evening, Ethan, my oldest son, and I sat on the deck, soaking in the last rays of the beautiful fall weather. We embarked on a conversation that lasted over an hour, built on the foundation of simply asking each other anything. We bounced back and forth with lighthearted questions like, "What's your funniest memory of me?" and "What are you most excited about for college life?" The entire conversation was filled with laughter and joy.

Then, Ethan hit me with a question that warmed my heart: "What do you admire most about me?" I loved it. My mind raced, searching for the perfect answer. Thoughts of "hard worker," "empathic," "generous," "loving," and "musically talented" all flitted through my mind, but none felt quite strong enough. After a few moments of contemplation, watching his anticipation grow, I said, "I love seeing your faith blossom and your passion for learning new things." His face lit up with joy at my answer. "Well," he replied, "you've made my faith journey fun and exciting." His words surprised me. At his age, I wouldn't have described my own faith walk as fun or exciting. But then again, I had no one to share it with.

The evening held more than just laughter and games. As I write, I'm navigating a season of personal health challenges. Back on August 13th, Ethan and I were pushing our limits at the gym with a trainer friend, tackling a brutal workout of box jumps, sled pushes, burpees, and sprints. Agility drills are my jam—fueling my drive to keep up with my kids, even push them a bit!

During that session, a subtle instability settled in my right knee. Ignoring it initially, the instability persisted, morphing into a dull ache as the workout progressed. I pushed on, fueled by my love for embracing physical discomfort. But on that day, I crossed a line, ignoring the clear messages my body was sending.

This experience highlighted a part of me, a tendency to embrace challenges to an extreme. While I cherish this drive, it needs balance. On that day, I learned a valuable lesson: listening to my body is crucial, even amidst the joy of pushing limits.

For over thirty years, fitness has been a cornerstone of my life. It's played a vital role, perhaps to an almost defining degree. At times, my identity and sense of self-worth have been closely tied to physical achievements and maintaining a certain image.

While fitness can be a powerful source of well-being, relying solely on it for self-worth can be precarious. When our physical appearance or athletic accomplishments become the sole measure of our value, we become vulnerable to fluctuations in self-esteem. Inevitably, fitness journeys have their ups and downs, from weight changes to performance plateaus. These natural shifts can trigger emotional turbulence and negatively impact mental health. A narrow focus on fitness as the core of who we are can create a cycle of self-criticism and disappointment when expectations aren't met.

Furthermore, prioritizing fitness exclusively can limit our self-perception and potential. By solely defining ourselves through physical attributes or athletic abilities, we may neglect other valuable aspects of our lives, such as relationships, intellectual pursuits, and emotional growth. This tunnel vision can lead to an imbalanced and incomplete understanding of self, hindering personal development and preventing us from embracing the richness and multidimensionality of our identities. In extreme cases, it can even contribute to feelings of inadequacy or worthlessness if fitness goals are not met, highlighting the potential dangers of placing too much emphasis on this single aspect of who we are. My health, fitness, and vitality were, I believed, paramount. Unfortunately, my own health was far from ideal. I remember thinking that if I couldn't train or maintain peak physical condition, who was I? Such an identity, whether built on work, fitness, or anything else, is a recipe for trouble. To add insult to injury, I'd been wrestling with a nasty injury. My knee joint had been hemorrhaging internally for ten weeks. The doctors were baffled, and everyone around me was worried. I was forced to swallow a large dose of humble pie, my health now a major question mark. I'd been in a funk for weeks, and the Internet, as it always does, was happy to offer up the worst-case scenarios imaginable when it came to my health concerns.

After our conversation on the deck, I retired to our bedroom, eager to crawl into bed and escape the throbbing pain in my knee. Lying there, I followed my routine of the past few weeks: scouring the web for the latest treatment and recovery videos, searching for potential causes and DIY solutions.

My online research quickly morphed into a descent into despair. I stumbled across countless articles and stories painting a grim picture. Patients with similar conditions, I read, were stuck with the bleeding forever, at risk of losing their limbs. My mind, flooded with overwhelming stress, anxiety, and fear, craved more information. But the deeper I dug, the more horrifying the images and stories became. This simple quest for treatment had become an endless journey into the abyss. I started imagining life without a leg. I regretted not playing with my boys more, not taking more trips that required the full use of my limbs. The sharp pang of regret struck me: I never learned to ski or snowboard with them. My mind was in full crisis mode.

That night, despair engulfed me with an intensity I'd never known. The cruel reality dawned: my physical life might be forever altered. My capabilities, potentially diminished for good. This insidious condition even threatened the very limb on which I stood. I broke. Tears streamed down my face, unbidden and relentless. A potent cocktail of sadness and anger churned within me. How unfair, I thought, how utterly undeserved this suffering.

As I lay there, face awash in uncontrolled tears, Ethan entered the room, his unexpected presence a jolt to my system. I scrambled to regain composure, to hide the rawness of my emotions. But it was too late. He saw it all. He sat beside me on the bed, his face a beacon of warmth and calm.

"Dad, are you okay?" he asked, his voice a gentle caress.

"Oh, yeah, buddy," I choked out, feigning normalcy as I brushed away the tears.

He smiled, radiating a peace that defied my turmoil. "No, you're not," he said softly, but with unwavering conviction.

"I'm scared, son," I confessed. "The pain is relentless, and no one seems to know how to fix it. I just need answers, some assurance that this will all be all right. But right now, there's none to be found."

"Dad," he said, his smile unwavering, "it will be all right. Would you mind if I prayed for you?"

Before I reveal the specifics of his prayer, I must describe the remarkable tableau that played out before me. My son, Ethan, sat perched on the edge of my bed, witnessing my vulnerability. The scene mirrored countless times I had sat beside him, offering comfort and guidance through his own struggles. In that moment, our positions were reversed. His unwavering smile, his comforting tone, his unwavering confidence—all conspired to create an atmosphere of profound peace. I say this without reservation: God was present in that room. A presence that permeated both Ethan and the space around us, a peace I had encountered only a handful of times in my entire life.

He reached for my left hand, cradling it gently between both of his. His eyes closed as he began to pray. "Father in heaven," he began, his voice a soothing balm, "please grant my father healing. Allow his body to mend and his mind to find solace. Assure him that answers will come, that he will not be left to wander in uncertainty. Grant him strength during this trial and remind him that he is not alone."

The words washed over me, each syllable carrying the weight of his faith and sincerity. I felt the undeniable presence of the Holy Spirit.

As Ethan's prayer concluded, his eyes slowly fluttered open. They met mine, and he saw the tears I could no longer restrain. These tears, however, were different. They were tears of pride, born from witnessing my son's strength and unwavering faith. He had offered me a spiritual lifeline, raising me up with his own belief. It was a moment of surrender, one of the most profound I had ever experienced. A part of me resisted, clinging to the ingrained paternal instinct to be the pillar of strength for my son. But I surrendered that impulse, recognizing this as his opportunity to take the lead, to lead with the knowledge and faith he had nurtured. It was an incredible act of grace, a testament to his own growth and strength.

Ethan and I exchanged a gift that night, one that will forever be etched in my memory. The awkwardness of surrendering to his request to pray over me was quickly eclipsed by the profound sense of reward. A surge of pride swelled within me, laced with the conflicting desire to shield him from the burden of praying for his ailing old man. Yet, refusing him would have been an unforgivable misstep. In denying him, I would have denied him the chance to forever cherish the memory of praying over his father, lifting him up in a moment of need.

In that moment, I witnessed not only the strength of my son's faith but also a glimpse into the future. I saw the father he would one day become, the calm, comforting presence he would offer his own children, the unyielding faith and confidence he would instill. It was a scene of exquisite beauty, a testament to the power of nurturing. As fathers, we pour our hearts and souls into our children's growth, yet rarely do we witness the fruits of our efforts. For that single, unforgettable moment, I was offered a glimpse of the man my son would become, forever grateful for the gift he bestowed upon me.

Nurturing our children's spiritual growth can seem like a daunting task, one that easily overwhelms us. But the truth is, it's a journey of both leadership and followership. We guide them through their formative years, offering our direction and wisdom. We allow them to lead when they are ready, fostering the growth of their own leadership skills. And we walk beside them, learning and growing alongside them. Nurturing, leading, and following—these are the intertwined threads that weave the tapestry of our children's faith journeys.

BEYOND THE MATERIAL: *FINDING TRUE FULFILLMENT AS FATHERS*

Dads, like all individuals, are often drawn to the seductive allure of material possessions, titles, money, and other outward markers of success. This obsession stems from a complex interplay of psychological, social, and cultural factors.

Social Comparison
We naturally compare ourselves to others, and this comparison can fuel a desire to acquire things that

demonstrate our worth and social standing. Titles and wealth often become symbols of success in such a competitive landscape.

Self-Esteem

Accumulating possessions and achieving high status can provide a much-needed boost to self-esteem. The validation and competence associated with these achievements can be immensely gratifying, serving as a balm to self-doubt.

Extrinsic Motivation

Some individuals are driven by external rewards, finding satisfaction in the tangible outcomes of their efforts. Money, promotions, and recognition are natural motivators for those who thrive on extrinsic validation.

Cultural and Social Norms

Our society often champions material success and the accumulation of wealth. Messages from media, advertising, and even our peers can subtly reinforce the belief that possessions and titles equate to happiness and fulfillment.

Security and Comfort

Financial security and the comfort it affords are often seen as cornerstones of a happy life. The ability to provide for ourselves and our loved ones can be a powerful motivator, driving us to pursue material success.

Social Status and Respect

Earning titles and achieving financial success often translates to increased social standing and respect within our communities. This recognition and admiration can be a significant motivator for some individuals.

Instant Gratification

Possessions and money can provide immediate gratification, offering a quick dopamine hit that can be difficult to resist. This short-term reward can often outweigh long-term considerations and lead to impulsive decisions.

However, it's crucial to remember that the significance individuals place on these material markers varies greatly. Not all men, or people in general, are driven by the same desires. Some find intrinsic motivation in personal growth, strong relationships, and meaningful experiences, valuing these aspects of life over material gains.

Understanding these psychological drivers can empower individuals to reflect on their values and motivations, allowing them to make conscious choices about what truly matters to them. In the context of fatherhood, prioritizing faith and values over material possessions can pave the way for a more fulfilling and meaningful life, both for fathers and their families.

Throughout my life, I've witnessed the extremes of this obsession, including instances where achieving the highest levels in certain areas brought no additional joy or fulfillment. Conversely, I've seen individuals (me, included) stripped of things deeply integrated into their identity, prompting a profound search for meaning after their loss. These experiences serve as a stark reminder that true fulfillment lies beyond the fleeting satisfaction of material possessions.

FROM RICHES TO REDEMPTION: *A FATHER'S TRANSFORMATION*

Some time ago, I received a coaching application from a man named Mike. Before our first meeting on Zoom, I delved into his application details. Mike, a "successful" business owner, had been married for fourteen years and was a father to three sons (ages ten, eight, and six). In his application, he expressed a desire to strengthen his connection with his wife and boys, acknowledging that his work had sometimes overshadowed his family life. This sentiment is quite common among my clients who are business owners, so nothing in Mike's application initially stood out to me. Yet the day we had our discovery call on Zoom—a session to explore the possibility of working together—turned out to be unforgettable, leaving an indelible mark on my memory and ensuring that I would always remember Mike.

When I started our Zoom meeting, I noticed Mike was already waiting, having joined five minutes early. Over the years, I've come to realize that those who arrive early to these calls are often deeply committed to personal growth. Welcoming him into the call, I noticed a mix of enthusiasm and weariness in his expression.

Mike, in his early forties, had an air of accomplishment. The backdrop of his office, neatly arranged and adorned with college degrees and various certificates, spoke volumes. Photos of his wife and three sons added a personal touch to the professional setting. Physically, Mike seemed fit and dedicated, the epitome of a hardworking individual. At first glance, he appeared to have it all—a testament to his achievements. However, my experience has taught me that appearances can be deceiving, and there's often more to a person's story than meets the eye.

Mike and I exchanged pleasantries for the first few minutes. Then his story unfolded around his business—a family legacy his father had started, which he later took over. He shared both the triumphs and challenges of running such a vast operation with numerous employees. He touched briefly on his family life with his three boys and wife, suggesting everything was fine, though there was an unspoken understanding between us that perhaps it wasn't. Then, he revealed something that made my heart race and momentarily took my breath away.

Curious, I asked Mike, "What brings you here today? Why do you want coaching?"

He paused, gathering his thoughts for what seemed like a significant revelation. After a deep breath, he said, "I just sold my company for 42 million dollars."

The magnitude of that figure was astounding. I've encountered millionaires in my career, but this was an exceptional milestone.

With genuine enthusiasm, I responded, "Congratulations! That's an incredible achievement! You must feel elated!"

He sighed deeply, struggling to contain his emotions. His head bowed as he tried to compose himself.

"You'd think I'd be overjoyed, and part of me feels I should be. But reflecting on what it cost me to reach this point, I'm not sure it was worth it."

Intrigued, I urged him to elaborate.

"The first thing my wife asked when I told her," he continued, "was whether this meant I could finally join in on 'Donuts with Dad' at the kids' school." As he shared this, he broke down, tears streaming down his face. I sensed there was more to his story, something deeply impactful.

"Larry, I've been working toward this my entire life, believing it was what my family wanted. I thought by working hard, I would create a lasting legacy and ensure they never worried about finances."

He paused, tears still flowing.

"But now, I realize my family hardly knows me. My sons don't really know their dad. My wife feels isolated, disconnected from her husband. My boys are young enough for me to make amends, and my marriage can still be mended. I've been chasing the wrong dream, not seeing what I've been missing. It's time for me to make a change."

Mike swiftly became not only a client but one of the most dedicated ones I've ever had.

From the outset, Mike immersed himself fully in our program. He consistently arrived first for every virtual group coaching session. My fellow coaches and I always felt a surge of enthusiasm when we'd start a Zoom session and find Mike eagerly waiting in the virtual lobby, ten minutes ahead of time. His approach was akin to an eager student in the front row, diligently taking notes and engaging with thoughtful questions. He was the kind of participant who absorbed every lesson with unmatched zeal.

Week by week, Mike consistently led our sessions with a positive update, sharing his progress and breakthroughs. He wasn't just learning; he was actively applying the lessons, a remarkable feat considering the demanding year he had spent finalizing his business sale. His communication with his wife improved significantly; he listened more deeply and was fully present in their interactions. His work no longer overshadowed his thoughts. His time with his sons was renewed—he was there for "Donuts with Dad" at school, creating cherished memories.

Mike's efforts were transforming his relationships in profound ways.

I'm pleased to share that Mike revolutionized his family life. He now spends quality, focused time with his boys and gives his wife the attention and connection she deserves. He openly admits that his former pursuit of titles, wealth, and material things was misguided. These pursuits had become so entwined with his identity, a common trap for many men. The danger lies in tying our sense of self to these external achievements. The real challenge surfaces when these worldly markers are lost or compromised, leaving us to confront the question of who we are without them.

DIAMONDS FROM DARKNESS: *FINDING STRENGTH IN TRAGEDY*

Life's toughest moments often reveal our most precious gifts, much like diamonds emerging from intense pressure. These adversities not only mold our character but can also cultivate enduring beauty in our communities and the wider world.

Viewed through a Christian lens, this concept resonates with the biblical principle of finding strength in weakness and God's work in challenging situations. In times of hardship, Christians draw on their faith to uncover resilience and grace. Just as individuals discover their true strength in adversity, the Christian belief highlights God's power to transform struggles into opportunities for growth and the unveiling of wonderful gifts, enriching life in line with God's divine plan.

In my years of meeting various clients, the stories I've heard have left a profound impact, particularly Mike's. His tale of remarkable financial and professional success, a rarity achieved by few, is etched in my memory. We often overlook the sacrifices that accompany such success. Mike's story is a poignant reminder of the risks involved in anchoring our identity to worldly achievements, which can jeopardize our most treasured family relationships. Ironically, in our pursuit to provide, we may end up neglecting what truly matters.

Similar to Mike, I encountered another unforgettable client in May 2018, a man named Mark. When I first reviewed his coaching application, nothing particularly stood out. Mark was seeking guidance and support to improve as a father and husband. Yet our initial meeting left an indelible mark on me, and to this day, Mark remains an integral member of our community. His journey and the inspiration he has spread are akin to a tidal wave of influence and motivation.

I remember starting our Zoom meeting and noticing Mark already waiting, a clear sign of his dedication. Observing him, I saw a man who took great care of himself. He was bald, sporting a five o'clock shadow, dressed in a shirt and tie. His office, located in downtown New York City, was meticulously organized. Before exchanging any pleasantries, I detected a certain intensity in Mark's gaze, indicating he was here for a deeply personal reason. His initial appearance was somewhat intimidating, projecting a tough and stoic demeanor. Yet there was something in his eyes that hinted at a vulnerability beneath his rugged exterior, a blend of resilience and an underlying sense of being weathered by life's challenges.

"Hello, Mark, it's great to finally meet you," I greeted him with a warm smile.

"Larry, good to meet you too. It's nice to put a face to the voice," Mark replied, his New York accent coloring his words. He smiled, but I sensed a heavy burden in his demeanor, a subtle hint of something more profound and unspoken.

We briefly chatted about work and fitness, sharing light-hearted exchanges. Mark, with his well-put-together appearance, mentioned his family: married for nineteen years, a father to three—Kyle, seventeen, and two daughters, Brooke, thirteen, and Paige, ten.

Curious, I inquired, "What brings you to seek coaching, Mark?"

There was a noticeable pause. I sensed the gravity of what he was about to share.

"I need support in my roles as a man, husband, and father," he said, pausing again, his gaze shifting away from the screen. The weight of his next words was palpable.

As he looked back at me, his eyes were brimming with tears, a struggle to maintain composure evident.

"Larry, I'm grappling with a father's worst fear," he paused, taking a moment to steady himself. "My daughter has been diagnosed with a rare, incurable cancer. We found out just a few weeks ago, on Mother's Day. The prognosis is that we'll lose her in a few months. There's nothing we can do."

Mark paused again, visibly gathering himself amidst the overwhelming revelation.

As Mark collected himself, I found myself also at a loss for words, overwhelmed by emotion. In my career, I've encountered many stories, but none as heart-wrenching as this. Witnessing Mark's helplessness in the face of such a devastating, uncontrollable situation was deeply humbling. The unimaginable nightmare of losing a child, a fear shared by every parent, was his stark reality.

Mark continued, his voice tinged with profound sorrow, "I've realized I can't navigate this dark valley alone. In the next twelve months, I'll lose my little girl. The anguish we've faced as a family is indescribable. There are days when I wake up hoping it was all a bad dream, only to be confronted with the harsh truth. I'm at a loss. I don't know how to support my wife, my other children, or even cope with this myself. The pain is simply unbearable."

I remained silent, simply offering my presence as a listener. In less than twenty minutes of knowing each other, Mark had laid bare the deepest, most vulnerable parts of his life. His raw display of fear and heartbreak was overwhelming. As he broke down, I found myself unexpectedly tearing up, deeply moved by his plight. His pain resonated with me, making me reflect on my own family and the unbearable thought of experiencing such a loss. Mark's grief was palpable, and despite my usual composure, his anguish echoed in me, a haunting reminder of the fragility of life.

Mark quickly became an active part of our community. Upon sharing his story, he received an outpouring of support from hundreds of men worldwide, all united in prayer and empathy for him and his family. This collective support played a crucial role in helping Mark navigate his darkest times. Remarkably, his journey, though filled with struggle, brought our community closer together. It was a profound reminder of the strength found in collective compassion and empathy, gifts that God has bestowed upon humanity.

In January 2019, Mark and his wife, Trish, faced the heartbreaking loss of their fourteen-year-old daughter, Brooke, to cancer. This tragedy deeply affected their family. Yet in the years that followed, Mark transformed his grief into a mission to support others facing similar challenges. He founded a nonprofit in Brooke's memory to aid families grappling with the loss of a child. Additionally, he launched a podcast to share his experiences, offering insights and strategies to help families cope during such trying times. Mark embraced what he saw as a higher calling, using his pain to bring light to others. His journey exemplifies how our deepest challenges can give rise to the most profound and beautiful contributions.

THE ETERNAL ANCHOR: *THE STEADFAST EMBRACE OF GOD'S LOVE*

At the heart of our Christian faith is the unshakable belief in God's unwavering love. This profound truth stands as a beacon of hope, reassuring us of God's steadfast and enduring love amidst life's trials. In the face of uncertainty, God's love is a firm foundation, offering us refuge and consistent affection. This promise is a source of comfort and strength, inviting us to find solace in the Creator's unchanging and boundless love, bringing peace and security amidst life's trials and tribulations.

Throughout my career, I've witnessed a myriad of life experiences. I've seen millionaires lose everything and yet others rebuild from the ashes. I've been alongside men as they've faced and overcome life-threatening challenges, while sadly, some have succumbed to them. Marriages have faltered and fallen apart, sometimes abruptly as couples give up on each other. Tragically, I've also seen fathers endure the unspeakable pain of losing children to accidents. However, there's also been light amidst the darkness—marriages that were on the brink of collapse have been revived and strengthened. I've seen families triumph over severe illnesses, and men who've lost their fortunes rise again to achieve new levels of success and financial independence.

The journey of life is inherently dynamic, marked by both highs and lows. We traverse through dark valleys, grappling with despair for weeks, months, or even years, and also experience heights of victory and success that seem unshakable. Life, in its essence, is a continuous flux, much like the stock market with its bear and bull phases.

Amidst this constant change, one steadfast element remains: God's unwavering love. While God never assured us a life devoid of problems or pain, God's promise of unchanging love is a constant. This love never wavers or falters. In a world where health, finances, marriages, and relationships can shift unpredictably, God's love stands as a perpetual and unyielding presence.

The Bible offers numerous verses that underscore this concept of God's eternal and steadfast love, illustrating its unwavering nature regardless of life's varying circumstances. These scriptures provide solace and reassurance, emphasizing the enduring nature of divine affection:

Psalm 136:26: "Give thanks to the God of heaven. *His love endures forever.*"

Psalm 136:1: "Give thanks to the LORD, for he is good. *His love endures forever.*"

Jeremiah 31:3: "The LORD appeared to us in the past, saying: 'I have loved you with an everlasting love; I have drawn you with unfailing kindness.'"

Romans 8:38–39: "For I am convinced that neither death nor life, neither angels nor demons, neither the present nor the future, nor any powers, neither height nor depth, nor anything else in all creation, will be able to separate us from the love of God that is in Christ Jesus our Lord."

1 John 4:9–10: "This is how God showed his love among us: He sent his one and only Son into the

world that we might live through him. This is love: not that we loved God, but that he loved us and sent his Son as an atoning sacrifice for our sins."

John 3:16: "For God so loved the world that he gave his one and only Son, that whoever believes in him shall not perish but have eternal life."

These verses highlight the eternal and unchanging nature of God's love, underscoring its constancy and steadfastness, irrespective of life's varying challenges and circumstances. This assurance of God's everlasting love offers comfort and uplifts those seeking solace and guidance in their faith journey. It is a message that brings hope and reassurance to believers.

ACKNOWLEDGMENTS

First, I would like to thank my wife, Jessica, for all her support since the inception of The Dad Edge mission that started in 2011. Without her unyielding support of me, this work, and the mission of helping men, husbands, fathers, and families, this mission would not have existed. You are the best mother and wife a man could ask for. Over the years, your faith has been my inspiration. When we first met in 1996, I had never developed a relationship with God. Seeing you so strong in your faith over the years has been a shining example of what it means to have a deep relationship with God.

Secondly, I would like to thank my four boys: Ethan, Mason, Lawson, and Colton, who gave me grace, patience, and time to write this book. All of you have inspired me to not only be a better man but also a better dad who continues to make mistakes.

Thank you for your grace and constant forgiveness. I would like to thank my editor, Phil Marino; without his help, this book would not be a reality. Thank you for helping me bring these stories and my words to life!

Appendix

A Father's Prayers

As we wrap up this book, I know I have sporadically given you some examples of prayers when you might need them most. I also know that being a busy dad and leader, we don't have the luxury of time to page through this entire book to find a prayer when you might need it most.

I also want to share some gratitude that you picked this book up and read through these pages with me. As you can see, I am still a student in all of this as well. If you are overwhelmed with the notion of deepening your connection with God, trust me, I was (and still am) right there with you. This is a journey. This is a journey that can feel overwhelming at times. However, I will tell you (and many of you probably already know this), it's a journey worth taking. It won't be perfect, but no journey is perfect. With any journey, there will be rough terrain, obstacles, challenges, and there will even be times we might lose the path and stray off. There will also be times of breathtaking beauty, successes, incredible insights, and a strengthening of the man, husband, and father we were called to be.

The Spirit of Fatherhood: A Prayer

Dear Heavenly Father,

In this journey of fatherhood, we seek your guidance and strength. As we embark on the journey of Fatherhood, help us find confidence as we prepare for this role. Grant us the courage to embrace the unknown and transform our anxieties into confidence. Teach us to balance our time between parenthood and personal pursuits, while aligning to our individuality.

As we pursue our spiritual growth, help us reflect on our spiritual identity as dads. May our prayers deepen the bond between us and our children, and may we find the strength to let go of past mistakes and nurture our souls as fathers. Guide us to celebrate our uniqueness and embrace personal growth, setting realistic expectations and finding encouragement in our fatherhood tribe.

Help us to forge unbreakable bonds with our children, teach us to be teachers of life, imparting wisdom, courage, and insight to our little ones. Help us cultivate unwavering loyalty, respect, and devotion in our relationships with our children. Nourish their independence while setting an example of true affection and heartfelt listening. Enable us to be pillars of support, always there for them in times of need, and empower them to blossom with compassionate confidence and limitless self-worth.

Help illuminate our purposeful paths, guide us to nurture the aspirations and growth of our children. Help us encourage their dreams through active listening and create a balance between discipline and controlled chaos. Provide them with opportunities to explore and cultivate their ethical and moral landscapes, so they may find purposeful paths in life.

Help us develop compassionate communication by helping us find the balance between honesty and empathy. Teach us to model effective family interactions and encourage authenticity and trust within our homes. Grant us the grace to face tough conversations with love and tenderness, embracing reflective honesty in ourselves and our relationships.

Enable us to use words that heal and strengthen family ties and create deep connections with our children through effective communication.

Guide us in creating a legacy of love. Help us find joy in life's simple gifts and understand the ripple effect of family faith beyond the pew. Guide us to embrace imperfections and lead with authentic spiritual leadership. Teach us the power of surrender through prayer and show us that true fulfillment as fathers goes beyond material possessions. Help us recognize the timeless treasures of faith, love, and virtues that are greater than money. Grant us the strength to find diamonds of strength in times of darkness and to recognize the authentic wealth that lies within.

We thank you, dear Father, for the gift of fatherhood and for the everlasting strength you provide. May we embrace the constants in life, knowing that you are always with us.

In your holy name, we pray.

Amen.

Prayer for Protection

Lord, I pray for the safety and protection of my family. Watch over us day and night, guarding us from harm, accidents, and danger. Surround us with Your angels and keep us safe in Your loving care. Amen.

A Prayer for Unity

Heavenly Father, help us, as a family, to walk in unity and love. Grant us the grace to support and uplift one another. May our home be a place of peace, harmony, and understanding. Amen.

A Prayer for Wisdom

Lord, grant us wisdom in our decisions and actions. Help us make choices that honor You and benefit our family's well-being. May Your guidance always lead us on the right path. Amen.

A Prayer for Gratitude

Thank You, Lord, for the gift of my family. I am grateful for each member and the love we share. Help me never to take them for granted and to express my love and appreciation regularly. Amen.

A Prayer for Forgiveness

Lord, grant us the ability to forgive and seek forgiveness within our family. Help us let go of grudges and misunderstandings, and may Your love and grace always prevail. Amen.

A Prayer for Spiritual Growth

Heavenly Father, I pray that each member of our family grows closer to You. May our faith deepen, and our relationship with You become more intimate with each passing day. Amen.

A Prayer for Joy and Laughter

Lord, fill our home with laughter and joy. Help us find delight in each other's company and create cherished memories together. Amen.

A Prayer for Health

Gracious God, I ask for Your healing touch upon the health of my family. Please grant us good physical and emotional health and protect us from sickness and harm. Amen.

A Prayer for Financial Blessings

Lord, provide for our family's needs and bless the work of our hands. Grant us wisdom in managing our finances, and help us be good stewards of the resources You've entrusted to us. Amen.

A Prayer for Marital Strength

Father, I pray for the strength and health of my marriage. Help me be a loving and supportive husband. May our marriage be a reflection of Your love for the Church. Amen.

A Prayer for Children

Lord, bless our children with health, wisdom, and a strong faith. Guide them as they grow, and may they become a source of joy and pride for our family and a blessing to others. Amen.

A Prayer for Guidance and Direction

Heavenly Father, grant our family clarity and direction in our goals and aspirations. May we seek Your will in all we do, and may You lead us on the path You have chosen for us. Amen.

A Prayer for Peace

Lord, grant our family peace that surpasses understanding. Help us trust in Your sovereignty, even in times of uncertainty or turmoil. May Your peace reign in our hearts and home. Amen.

A Prayer for Thankfulness

Thank You, Lord, for the gift of family. I thank You for each member and the love we share. Help me never to take them for granted and to express my gratitude to You continually. Amen.

A Prayer for a Heart of Service

Lord, teach me to serve my family with a humble heart, just as Christ served the Church. May I lead by example in acts of love, kindness, and selflessness. Amen.